An Introduction to
BALLET

An Introduction to
BALLET

Compiled by
Craig Dodd

with features by

Ann Nugent

CHARTWELL
BOOKS, INC.

For Mona Vangsaae

Acknowledgments

My greatest thanks go to Ann Nugent for her major contributions to this book. Indeed, without her it would have been impossible for me to complete it or do the research necessary for the features on schools and syllabuses (which she would have been much happier to call 'syllabi') on which she spent so much time.

As with all my previous books various friends in the ballet world have been particularly helpful in providing information and photographs. Clive Boursnell readily made available his vast collection of photographs of the Royal Ballet at work, many more of which can be found in his own magnificent book, *The Royal Opera House, Covent Garden*. Linda Rich spent more time than I could have reasonably expected in photographing the Royal Ballet School, in particular the students taking part in Mona Vangsaae's production of *Konservatoriet*. I am also extremely grateful to James Monahan and Barbara Fewster for agreeing to the story about the school and for making their facilities so readily available. Similarly my thanks to London Festival Ballet and the London Coliseum for allowing us the freedom of the house to photograph *At the Ballet*.

Craig Dodd

© 1983 Winchmore Publishing Services Limited

First published in the USA by Chartwell Books Inc.,
A Division of Book Sales Inc.,
110 Enterprise Avenue, Secaucus,
New Jersey 07094

ISBN 0 89009 535 3

Produced by Winchmore Publishing Services Limited
40 Triton Square
London NW1 3HG
England

Designed and picture-edited by Craig Dodd
Typeset by SX Composing Limited
Printed and bound by Graficromo s.a., Cordoba, Spain

Title page: Anthony Dowell as the Prince in Frederick Ashton's *Cinderella*.

Contents

Introduction

In compiling the different stories and sections which make up this book my main intention is to try to offer sound advice to young ballet students or those of you who might just be thinking about starting dance classes. I hope that some of the stories provide an amusing and interesting glimpse of backstage life, as well as the daily routine of a professional dancer. If you have decided to make a career in dancing, you will really have to dedicate your life. The glamour and excitement of performance is balanced by the daily grind in the studio, both in class and rehearsal. You will find both illustrated here, showing the strain and exhaustion of the exercises and the fun or boredom of rehearsals.

Not all of you will want to take up dancing as a career, but even for students who are dancing for the sheer pleasure it gives them, it is essential that care should be given to the choice of both school and teacher. I hope that you will find some helpful hints.

In preparing this book I have been greatly helped by Ann Nugent. At a time when I was unable to do further research she undertook far more work than originally intended and it is to her that you should be grateful for the carefully researched information on schools and syllabuses, as well as the 'behind the scenes' look at life at the Royal Ballet School.

It was always my wish to dedicate this book to a great ballerina and friend, Mona Vangsaae, the original Juliet in Sir Frederick Ashton's *Romeo and Juliet*. Sadly, just as the book was completed, she died. This makes her appearance in the chapter on the Royal Ballet School, which was where she spent one of the happiest periods of her life, a last tribute to a very special lady.

Craig Dodd

At the Ballet

The best introduction to the world of ballet is to see a performance of a classic ballet by one of the world's great companies, if possible in an historic theatre. This is what was arranged for Emma-Louise, who takes ballet classes at the Royal Academy of Dancing in London.

Apart from the enjoyment and excitement of the performance, you now see what all your hard work in the ballet studio is for. It shows that the daily strain of working your body and improving technique is aimed at creating an instrumen t to express the dance and the characters effortlessly on th e stage.

Ballet, more than opera or drama, needs live performances. Although you can see more, and much better produced, ballet on the television nowadays, it does not have the same impact as when you see it on the stage. No amount of collecting photographs of your favourite dancers, keeping a scrapbook or, if you are lucky, building up a library of video tapes, can take the place of actually watching the magic of the dance on stage.

For our evening at the ballet we were fortunate to be invited to see John Field's new production of *Swan Lake* for London Festival Ballet, of which he is now the Director. It was specially created for the large stage of the London Coliseum theatre and at this performance the role of Odette/Odile was to be danced by Andria Hall, partnered by Ben van Cauwenburgh as Prince Siegfried.

London Festival Ballet has had a much shorter life than the famous Coliseum, where it gives regular London seasons. The Coliseum, home of the English National Opera, has had a long and varied history. It has housed opera and operetta, music hall and films. Many great ballet stars have danced there over the years since it opened on 24 December 1904.

Sir Oswald Stoll decided to build a great music hall on the site near Trafalgar Square. He employed Frank Matcham, the greatest designer of theatres of his day, to design it. Started in 1903, by the end of 1904 its great tower, on which stand four figures representing Art, Music, Science and Architecture, topped by a revolving globe, was a London landmark.

Sir Oswald was very keen on dance and from the earliest days many famous dancers were associated with it. The Danish ballerina Adeline Genée, who made her home in Britain, performed regularly and gave her farewell performance there in 1914. In true theatre tradition she made many come-backs until

Two old posters from the London Coliseum; Adeline Genée appears alongside the Victoria Troupe of Expert Lady Trick and Acrobatic Cyclists and Karsavina next to the Trills and Frills of the McConnell Sisters. Next week's attractions include Lydia Lopokova dancing with Leonide Massine.

1933 when she danced for the last time partnered by the young Anton Dolin. Dame Adeline, as she became, was one of the founders of the Royal Academy of Dancing.

Sir Oswald offered a London season to Serge Diaghilev who refused, saying that his great company could not dance surrounded by performing dogs and a fat lady playing a silver trombone. Years later, though, he did agree and the poster for the season announced the Entire Diaghilev Ballet Company alongside a comic act, Nervo and Knox, doing Fantastic Frolics. It is interesting to see that the price of an orchestra stall seat was two shillings and sixpence! That is twelve and a half pence (twenty cents) today, but you did have to pay an extra two and a half pence (four cents) if you reserved your ticket in advance!

London Festival Ballet is a relatively new company compared to some of the world's great companies such as the Paris Opera Ballet or the Kirov Ballet in Leningrad. It is less than half the age of the Royal Ballet, though, having been founded in 1950, it is almost the same age as the New York City Ballet. It grew into a company from a small group of dancers headed by Dame Alicia Markova and Sir Anton Dolin, both of whom had also taken part in the early years of the Royal Ballet in the 1930s, when it was known as the Vic-Wells Ballet. For many years it has been one of the world's great touring companies, having no permanent theatre of its own. Over the years it has introduced many outstanding foreign dancers to British audiences both in London and in most other major towns and cities. Each year it gives a Christmas season of *The Nutcracker* at London's Royal Festival Hall, as well as a regular Spring season at the Coliseum. The big classic ballets such as Mary Skeaping's production of *Giselle* or Peter Schaufuss's production of *La Sylphide* look particularly handsome on its spacious stage. It is a marvellous theatre for ballet as the sight-lines, the position of the seats, give a wonderfully clear and unobstructed view of the whole stage.

Emma-Louise arriving at the London Coliseum with posters featuring two young stars of London Festival Ballet, Lucia Truglia and Matz Skoog.

Even buying a programme can be exciting and there are always plenty of other interesting things to look at at the bookstall.

A chance meeting with Antoinette Sibley and an autograph for Emma-Louise.

On the way to the restaurant before the performance. Even the staircases at the Coliseum are particularly elegant. ▶

The first problem if you want to attend a performance, which did not arise this time, is buying a ticket! Ballet, especially the big classic ballets danced by international stars, is now big business and very successful at the box office. It can be expensive. If you live outside London this can make for a very costly evening when you add up the price of the tickets for the performance, the cost of travel and a meal or refreshment. However it is still worth saving up for that special occasion. It would, of course, be nicer if tickets were cheaper and more easily available, but without much more money from the government, this is very unlikely. Throughout Europe it is possible to subscribe to the ballet performances, just as you might do for your favourite magazine. This means that you can have a seat regularly on the nights you have subscribed for at a reduced rate. This may sound a marvellous idea, but has its problems. Often you have to attend a performance surrounded by people who have subscribed and do not really want to be there on that particular night. Their lack of enthusiasm is soon obvious to those around them, as well as to the dancers, which makes for a very dull evening.

Arriving at the theatre has an excitement of its own; the posters, the photographs, the lights, the bustling crowd on the pavement waiting to get in. Once inside the theatre there are photographs of other productions to look at, perhaps featuring some of your favourite ballet stars. The latest dance books and magazines are on display at the bookstall alongside a whole range of postcards and posters of dancers and endless souvenirs of the theatre itself. It is even possible that in the crush of people you might see some famous dancers as they never seem to tire of watching ballet performances. It might even be an opportunity to get an autograph or two.

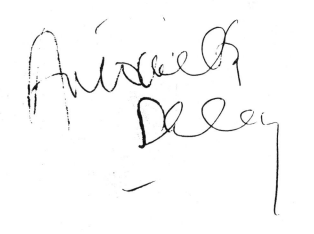

If it is a 'story' ballet which you are seeing and you are not completely familiar with it, it helps to read the programme note. Sometimes, even if you *think* you know it, it might help to do this, as producers sometimes change even the most familiar and famous stories. It is very important that once you have settled down in your seat you relax and enjoy the dance and not worry too much about details of the story, or what particular actions *mean*. It is the movement itself which matters most.

As the auditorium fills up there is always an expectant hush when the lights start to dim and the conductor is at his place. Then darkness and with a rush the curtains part to reveal a magnificent, very realistic setting for the first act of *Swan Lake*.

A last minute look at the programme before curtain up.

Look around! Some old theatres can be as fascinating as the ballet.

During the interval it is always interesting to explore the theatre itself, including the bar or restaurant. The design of many of the grand old theatres can be a show in itself. The ceilings are usually full of fascinating detail, colour and interest. So many people look no higher than the stage and miss the art which has gone into painting some fanciful scene on the ceiling or carving a piece of sculpture, such as the lions and the portraits of Roman Emperors in the Coliseum. Sadly, many of the wonderful chandeliers have been removed to make way for modern stage lighting. Look out for the 'follow-spot' which now beams out of the ceiling in the Royal Opera House. The designs of these grand theatres often tell you something about the people who built them and those they were built for. The Royal Opera House in Copenhagen is quite small and rather plain as, when it was built, Copenhagen was a tiny city far removed from the main world of theatre. The mighty Kirov in Leningrad shows the importance of the Tsar, while the Paris Opera is perhaps the grandest of all, reflecting the French love of show. Most modern opera houses, such as those in Germany, are rather dreary places by comparison and have little theatrical atmosphere.

At the bar, not the barre! In the light suit by Emma-Louise is Dimitri Papoutsis whose outstanding talents as an osteopath have helped to keep many famous dancers on the stage.

The orchestra and a helpful musician.

◀ Curtain calls.

After this performance we were able to go backstage for a few moments to meet Andria and Ben. Andria Hall is one of London Festival Ballet's brightest young ballerinas, and one who grew up in the company after joining the corps de ballet in 1974. She is a particularly beautiful dancer with a wide range of roles, being equally good as a comic character in *Graduation Ball* or in a classic role full of great drama such as Odette in *Swan Lake*. Her partner, Ben van Cauwenburgh, comes from a famous Belgian dancing family. His brother is a well-known dancer, one aunt directs a ballet company and another a school! He is particularly good in the classic 'Prince' roles requiring great elegance and style.

Rushing backstage we were able to take a back view of the curtain calls and to see how quickly the stage staff had cleared the stage. They had already set up some of the barres ready for class the next day before the curtain calls were over.

A quick kiss for Andria from an old friend – the author.

Beryl Grey demonstrates for Andria and then signs an autograph for Emma-Louise.

By chance on this occasion, Beryl Grey, the great ballerina and former Director of London Festival Ballet, was backstage chatting to dancers and giving Andria some helpful advice about the performance. An opportunity for Emma-Louise to add another autograph to her collection.

With a jump our Prince heads for his dressing room.   Andria makes her way to her dressing room in rather more dignified fashion.

Curtain calls and helpful hints over, Andria and Ben made their way back to their dressing rooms. Once there Andria showed Emma-Louise the messy business of trying to disentangle the head-dress from her hair; a head-dress which had sparkled so beautifully from the stage, but now looked rather dull, drab and practical. Then there was the even messier business of removing the heavy stage make-up. This unglamorous end to a glamorous evening tells us a lot about the ballet; the hard work and dedication, often in bad conditions, which go into creating the perfect picture we see on the stage.

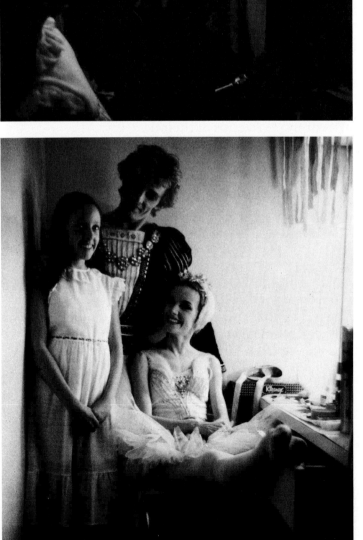

A last souvenir.

After a journey backstage at the ballet where you can appreciate a little of what goes into a performance, it will be interesting to take a journey even further back to see what went into the making of the dancers from the start of their ballet training. At whatever age someone takes up dancing, even if just for pleasure, one of the most important things is . . .

Choosing a School...

Choosing a good ballet teacher should not, in theory, be difficult but in practice it often is. There are still too many inadequate or even bad teachers to assume that the nearest will do, so unless you hear of one through personal recommendation, a certain amount of investigation is needed. Children's physical (and mental) progress is too important to be left to chance.

Look for the names of schools in the local paper, talk to other parents at your child's school, ask for suggestions at your library. Contact one of the well-known examining bodies such as the Royal Academy of Dancing or the Imperial Society of Teachers of Dancing, to see whether they can recommend a teacher. Or look for names in magazines on dance. In Britain, for example, the *Dancing Times* has a special section for reports from qualified teachers. Then go and watch a class before committing yourself.

Ballet in its early stages should be fun and invigorating. Children need straightforward classes that are designed simply to develop rhythmic co-ordination, good posture and a lively imagination. Teachers who pay attention to poised heads and the line of back and shoulders, who correct protruding tummies and bottoms, who insist on legs with pulled up knees and pointed feet are the ones to look out for. Avoid those who do not correct round shoulders, hollow backs, weak knees, sloppy feet and so on.

Notice whether the teacher and her pupils are neatly dressed. Grooming is an essential part of ballet, even at the most junior level, and an untidy class is an immediate giveaway. Observe, too, whether the child is encouraged to listen and respond to the music.

One of the major difficulties in ballet teaching is that some of the teachers who have impressive initials after their names, may have gained these years ago and by now have lost touch with current thinking. Ballet is continually developing as new theories in training are evolved using the latest scientific discoveries, and any good teacher should regularly attend official congresses or assemblies to keep in touch. This is assuming that she is registered with an examining body, but of course not all teachers are and you will have to be extra vigilant when assessing a teacher without obvious qualifications.

Many schools present their pupils in an annual summer performance, and this of course is another good way of assessing the quality of work. It is preferable to see children happily engrossed in simple patterns of runs and skips, than attempting complicated steps beyond their capabilities. It takes no specialist knowledge to realize that a child looks ill at ease when something is too difficult.

No teacher who allows young girls to balance insecurely on the tips of their toes, is worth considering. Since children are so different it is hard to generalize, but 11 is probably the earliest that a girl should be introduced to simple pointe work, and then only if she has had at least three years' careful training, which has given her a correct body placement, and strengthened legs, ankles and feet. Toes after all were not designed to take the body's full weight!

If a child shows real promise and enthusiasm (as opposed to a whim that will soon run its course) it may be worth continuing the training more seriously at a professional ballet school which could mean living away from home. This is not a step to be taken lightly for youthful promise does not always fulfil itself and decisions generally have to be made before a child is mature enough to know his or her own mind fully. Apart from the obvious benefits of a first-class training at a full-time ballet school (where a sound education is also provided), the aspiring young dancer will gain much from developing in professional surroundings. However, it is possible for a child to work towards a professional career with an exceptionally good local teacher, though it is usually advisable to move to a professional school at 16.

Most of the world's major ballet companies have important schools attached to them. In Britain The Royal Ballet School trains dancers for The Royal

Ballet, while in the United States, the School of American Ballet provides recruits for New York City Ballet. Similarly American Ballet Theatre, the Paris Opera Ballet, the Royal Danish Ballet, the Stuttgart Ballet, the Australian Ballet, the Canadian National Ballet, and the Kirov and Bolshoi Ballet Companies in Russia all have important schools backing them. From the hundreds of students who study at these schools only a handful graduate into the companies, the rest have to look for work elsewhere because they have not reached the required peak of excellence. Or because there are simply no vacancies.

Children are usually accepted into ballet schools at 11; occasionally at 12 or 13, except in Australia where they continue with local teachers until 16. By 11 most children will have some training with a reputable teacher. Bad training takes years to undo! Entry is by audition, when the successful candidate is expected to show natural dance ability, musicality, an alert manner and a healthy, strong and supple physique.

Additionally the child will need to have determination, stamina enough not to question the demands that are made, courage and the temperament to withstand both the knocks and the competition. There is an old saying that 'it takes blood, sweat and tears to make a dancer'. Make no mistake, ballet is tough. For the really gifted it is also, on occasions, inestimably rewarding.

If the child has a gift for movement, but lacks the physical perfection of the true classicist, a school that offers a broader theatre training may prove more suitable. In Britain there are several such schools that take youngsters of secondary-school age. They are all independently run and, more often than not, residential. Among the best known are the Bush Davies School at East Grinstead, Elmhurst Ballet School at Camberley, the Arts Educational Schools at Tring and, for day pupils and students only, London. Students graduating from these schools have a versatile background in classical and contemporary dance, tap, modern stage or jazz for older students, drama, voice-production, singing and so on, making them well equipped to cope with the varied demands of today's choreographers. The schools provide a sound education as well.

Entry is by audition, and there are always more applicants than places. All the reputable schools are accredited by the Council for Dance Education and Training, which serves as a guide to local authorities when considering requests for grant aid. But grants to recognized schools are awarded on a discretionary, not mandatory basis, and some authorities are very tight fisted. This can lead to difficulties in the case of parents who cannot afford the fees, although most schools offer occasional scholarships, and will do everything they can to help and advise the really talented aspirant.

In other countries nearly all professional ballet training is paid for by the state, except in the United States where very often committees are needed to raise funds for fees. There are no real equivalents to the British residential system of theatre training though similar courses of study are run – notably by the well-known High School of Performing Arts in, and funded by, New York City.

Marion Tait and Roland Price in Kenneth MacMillan's ballet *The Invitation*.

Once the choice of school has been decided, work starts in earnest in the studio. Different schools teach different styles and enter their students for different examinations. Most will follow the course of one of the three most important organizations, though there are others such as the British Ballet Organization. Here is a little background information about . . .

Your Syllabus

Exams do not make a dancer, and many of the world's greatest stars have never taken one in their life. Nevertheless they can serve a useful purpose, by providing a way to assess standards, as well as ensuring a properly constructed method of training. This is why they are important to many thousands of children and their teachers.

Today there are many different syllabuses and styles of training, among which are the three major international methods. Coincidentally all three were formed in the 1920s, and were organized into London-based societies. Originally the methods contained individual characteristics and differed greatly in examination standards, but over the years there has been a levelling out as the leading examiners from all three organizations have had long, formal discussions to try and build a unity between the syllabuses. Nowadays, for example, a student passing the Advanced Examination of the Royal Academy of Dancing, and another passing the Advanced Examination of the Cecchetti Society, may be said to be of similar standard whereas previously the Cecchetti Examination was very much harder. Now its old Advanced Syllabus has become the Enrico Cecchetti Diploma; the Intermediate Syllabus has been renamed Advanced, the Elementary, Intermediate, and a revised syllabus has taken the place of the former Elementary. In all methods the Elementary, Intermediate and Advanced syllabuses are known as 'major' examinations, and are intended for serious students who are perhaps thinking of taking ballet up professionally, as dancers or teachers. Before these come graded examinations for children, which are naturally far simpler in their approach.

The Royal Academy of Dancing

Of the organizations, the Royal Academy of Dancing is the largest and most widely known throughout the ballet world. It was founded in 1920, when it was known as the Association of Operatic Dancing, and it was granted the Royal Charter in 1936. By the 1910s, dancing in England had long been popular, but the emphasis was more on folk and social dance and many of the most respected ballet dancers were visitors from Europe. In 1912, Diaghilev brought his ballet company to London, and overnight a new interest in ballet was born.

Ballet teaching in Britain though was a sorry affair. The *Dancing Times* drew frequent attention to the shortfalls like poor standards of teaching and lack of organized development. After the First World War the magazine's then editor, Philip Richardson, decided that something had to be done to remedy this situation. There were at that time in England five leading dancers, representing the foremost European schools. Richardson persuaded them to come together and share their training methods, and so through Adeline Genée (Danish School) Tamara Karsavina (Russian School), Lucia Cormani (Italian School), Edouard Espinosa (French School) and Phyllis Bedells (English School), the Royal Academy of Dancing was born.

From those early influences, as the method was built up and improved on, the RAD grew into an international organization. It now receives almost 140,000 examination entries annually from all over the world. It also organizes many other events.

A Scholarship Scheme exists in Britain, enabling specially selected children to have regular weekly ballet classes free of charge with a particular scholarship teacher. These classes are intended to complement the child's regular teaching. Similar schemes are also run in Australia, New Zealand and South Africa. An annual Children's Summer School for 9 to 12 year-olds is held in London, where there is additionally an International Summer School for students and teachers. Annual Overseas Summer Schools are also organized, in a different country each year.

Students who do exceptionally well in their Advanced Examination, or who gain the final Solo Seal examination, may enter for the annual Adeline Genée Awards. These were started in 1931, and many gold medalists such as John Gilpin, Rowena Jackson, Bryan Ashbridge, Doreen Wells and Brenda Last, went on to outstanding careers, just as younger winners such as Nicola Katrak, Ravenna Tucker, Roland Price and Leanne Benjamin are also now making names for themselves.

The Genée Gold Medal (sponsored at present by the Imperial Group Limited) is awarded as acknowledgement of achievement, while the Bursary in Honour of Phyllis Bedells (also sponsored by the Imperial Group) is given to a young dancer of Intermediate level who shows real potential. Prize money of £1,000 has to be spent specifically on further training, but the Bursary has only existed in its present form since 1981, and so it is too early to say how it has affected its first two winners, Muriel Valtat and Errol Pickford.

The President of the RAD is Dame Margot Fonteyn, who was responsible for most of the syllabus for children's examinations. For those who outgrow children's work, and who wish to continue dancing at a less strenuous level than major exam work, there is an additional Dance Education Syllabus covering classical and character dance.

The Cecchetti Method

It was only because the English critic and historian Cyril Beaumont sensed the value of the great Cecchetti's teaching, that the method has been passed on. He undertook to commit it to paper, with help at first from the dancer Stanislas Idzikowski, and later from Cecchetti himself. At times, Beaumont wrote, 'the difficulties seemed insuperable', as he laboured day and night for more than two years on what was 'almost a Sisyphean task'. Finally the Cecchetti Method (outlining the careful build-up over days, weeks and years of study) was published in 1922 in *A Manual of Classical Theatrical Dancing* and the Cecchetti Society was formed. Eight years later Beaumont, with help from the teacher Margaret Craske, published more of Cecchetti's work in *The Theory and Practice of Allegro in Classical Ballet*.

Enrico Cecchetti was renowned first as a dancer, later as a mime and teacher. He was born in Italy in 1850, and died there in 1928, having travelled extensively in Europe during his career. He trained as a dancer under Giovanni Lepri, who in turn had been taught by Carlo Blasis, whose *Treatise on the Dance* (1820) and *The Code of Terpsichore* (1828) serve as the base on which classical ballet training has been built. Cecchetti developed his teaching from Blasis' work, and from his wide experience of the different schools of the time. In the latter part of the 19th century he was engaged as premier danseur and ballet master at St Petersburg (now Leningrad). Among his many created roles, undoubtedly performing both the mimed part of the Carabosse and the virtuoso Bluebird in *The Sleeping Beauty* was a highlight. He became ballet master of the Diaghilev Company at its formation in 1909, and exerted enormous influence throughout the ballet world during his nine years there. Then in 1918 he opened a school of dancing at 160 Shaftesbury Avenue in London. He returned to Italy in 1923, but though tired and suffering from ill health, his popularity was so great that his pupils followed him and demanded classes to the end.

The Cecchetti Method has a rich vocabulary that has adjusted, but not altered much over the years. It is the distillation of everything Cecchetti learned and he had an almost visionary understanding of movement. It is linked to the early classics, and contains such harmony, flow and exceptionally beautiful ports de bras (arm movements), that many teachers are passionate advocates of it.

The Cecchetti Society runs its own Summer School, and two important awards, the Cyril Beaumont Scholarship to the Royal Ballet Upper School, and the Mabel Ryan Awards, for juniors under 13, and seniors from 13 to 15.

In 1924, the Cecchetti Society amalgamated with the Imperial Society of Teachers of Dancing, as one of the 10 different branches of dance. The others include Greek, Historical, National and Modern Theatre Dance, Scottish Country and Highland Dancing, Ballroom Latin American and Sequence Dancing. However, also under the Classical Ballet wing comes the Imperial Society Syllabus, and this is the third method of study in this brief survey.

The Imperial Society

It was founded in 1924 by a group of teachers under the chairmanship of Jessie Hogarth, and while it has developed since, the original syllabus was identical to the RAD syllabus. Adeline Genée, the RAD's founder Chairman, gave permission for its use by the Imperial Society.

Although in essence, and as already indicated, Imperial Ballet does not differ substantially from the other two methods, in examinations dance quality is of paramount importance. While a child who is technically strong may do well in RAD examinations, one who has a true sense of dance and an instinctive musical response (but whose techniques may be less secure) may do better with Imperial Ballet.

The Imperial Ballet no longer has scholars, but it offers annual awards which provide funds for further approved tuition, and it also holds regular refresher courses and congresses. Like the RAD it has a large following throughout the world.

Addresses for further information are on page 96.

Once in a school you start to learn what hard work really is! At first you will be taught the simplest steps, but it is useful to know a little about what you are aiming for and will do if you persevere and perhaps become a professional dancer. Here is an idea in words and pictures of the many steps which go to make up a full...

Ballet Class

You cannot learn how to dance from a book, however clever and clear the words or beautifully posed the photographs. You can see certain positions clearly, you can see how static poses should look if done perfectly. What you cannot find out is how the body feels while doing these steps or holding these positions or, very importantly, understand the rhythm of the movement of each exercise.

What a book can do is provide you with a reminder of the steps in between your classes or give you some hints about how other dancers approach their daily class. For exact instructions and corrections you must always follow your teacher who will be guiding you along your chosen syllabus.

In describing a basic daily class, the sort of class a professional dancer might expect to do every day, I will try to give you some idea of what you are working towards. Many of the steps will not yet be part of your training and might not be for some years to come, others you might just be trying for the first time. The big jumps and multiple pirouettes, even pointe work, may also lie in the future, but the following descriptions will at least explain them to you in advance.

A last word of warning. Some steps, in particular some ports de bras, may not be exactly as you have been taught in your syllabus. I have described a general style made up of many different schools, so do not be confused if a particular detail is not as you are being regularly taught.

Before starting the class proper we should look at the basic positions of the body which are named after the five basic positions of the feet. These positions were not simply thought up by some clever teacher. They developed from the formal walking which made up court dance in the early years of ballet and were first written down by the teacher Beauchamp in the 17th century. Although toes would be elegantly turned out, the feet and legs would not have the sort of turn-out from the hips you see today.

Turn-out has a more practical basis than just looking elegant. As it comes from the hip joint (and *definitely* does not mean just having your feet turned out) the leg can move in a greater arc and out to the side. Can you imagine a stage performance of dance in which the leg could only move normally, up and down to the front? It would mean that the dancers would always have to have their bodies sideways to the audience!

For **First Position** you should have your legs together and your heels should be touching with the feet forming a straight line. While standing in this position you should stand straight and feel your body raising from your hips, breathing from your diaphragm to fill your lungs well.

In **Second Position** you should have your feet apart by about one and a half times the length of your foot, with the weight of your body balanced evenly.

Learning **Third Position** properly is a necessary step towards learning fifth position. You should bring your feet back together so that while still turned out the heel of one foot fits into the hollow of the instep of the other.

There are two versions of **Fourth Position**; open will come first, followed by crossed. In the open position you will have your feet almost in the same position as first, but with one foot about 12 inches in front of the other. In the crossed position your feet will look as though they are in fifth, but again with one foot in front of the other.

The most difficult to achieve is **Fifth Position**, but as you work gradually from third you will be aiming to have the heel of one foot against the toe of the other, without forcing turn-out from the ankles or knees.

The way the arms are held are called the **ports de bras** and as much care should be given to working with the arms properly as to any other part of the class. They should always be as relaxed and natural as possible with the line of the arm continuing through to the tip of the middle finger. The positions of the arms match the different positions of the feet, but this is an area where there are variations between the different syllabuses.

In general you could say that in **First Position** both your arms should be curved down naturally in front of you with the fingers held just a few inches apart to give a rounded shape from the shoulders down; for **Second Position** your arms will be held out to the side at a natural shoulder height, softly curving, with no nasty angle at the elbows, and relaxed hands held with the palm turned forward; for **Third Position** one arm will be in first position, the other in second; for **Fourth Position** one arm remains in second position, while the other is raised in a natural curve above the head and for **Fifth Position** both arms will be raised above the head with your elbows curved slightly and the hands a few inches apart.

The way you hold your shoulders, neck and head is called **épaulement**. Good bearing is very important and the head must be held in a good position to complement the rest of the pose.

Your ballet class will start with work at the barre and will aim to warm up the body progressively, preparing your muscles for the more difficult steps to follow. However, you should also take the precaution of doing some warming up exercises of your own before you start. Perhaps your teacher has already advised you about this as it is an extra safeguard against sprains or other injuries. Sometimes professional dancers cheat a little and use lots of leg warmers, but this is definitely not advisable for the young student.

As you will know every exercise at the barre will be done 'both sides', in other words each leg in turn will be the supporting leg and the working leg to give you balanced training.

Work at the barre starts with the **Pliés**, supporting yourself by holding the barre lightly and not gripping it tightly as this will simply cause you strain and also give you a false sense of balance. *Pliés* take their name from the French for 'bend' as they consist of a movement slowly lowering the body while bending the knees. They are intended to prepare your legs for the following exercises as well as helping improve

Students at the Royal Ballet School beneath a photograph of Prima Ballerina Assoluta, Margot Fonteyn

your turn-out. When lowering the body you must always remember to keep your back straight and your hips level, with the weight of your body balanced evenly between your feet. Your bottom must not stick out! The movement up and down should be smooth and even, as though you are working against a very strong spring. Your heels must be kept on the floor when you do *pliés* in second position, but can be allowed to rise naturally in first, third and fifth positions, the point when you feel the pressure for them to rise being the *demi-plié*.

After doing *pliés* in different positions you move on to **Tendus** which is an exercise consisting of the stretching of the leg and foot from a closed position to an open position and back, your toe never leaving the floor. This exercise helps develop fast footwork for the later allegro exercises, just as do the **Glissées**. During these your foot and leg glide (which is what it means) but this time your toe is allowed to leave the floor by about two inches, being the last to leave it and the first to return. This way the foot is always nicely pointed showing a good instep.

Moving on to **Ronds de Jambes á Terre** your legs are worked in a circular action rather than just back and to. You draw a semi-circle on the floor with the working leg, feeling the movement come from the hip, starting from first to fifth positions. Now that

your legs are starting to warm up and progressively move more freely you will move on to **Battements Frappés**. *Frapper* means to strike and that gives you some idea of the feeling of the movement. They are fast and sharp and the ball of your foot will brush the floor briefly as the leg swings, not in a complete arc from front to back, but from a closed position front or back to an open one and back again sharply.

Fondus are exercises working to progress towards the exercises which raise the leg right off the ground (so far your foot has never been more than a few inches away from it) and warm the muscles up further. The basic exercise consists of slowly raising one leg, from a *cou de pied* position, to an *attitude* forward, slowly doing a *demi-plié* as it is stretched out straight. For the first time in your exercises one leg will be carrying the whole weight of your body while in *plié*. This is an exercise which is going to help with the take-off for jumps as well as the beautifully soft landings that are so necessary.

Now that the working leg is moving freely in the air, it will start to work even harder. During **Ronds de Jambes en l'Air** your leg, or at least the lower half of it will make a circle in the air. Your working leg is raised so that your knee is almost at right-angles to your body. The foot then makes a circular motion (more of an oval than a true circle) in the air. This

exercise later appears in centre work and can best be seen in Bournonville ballets such as *Flower Festival* pas de deux when it is performed while the dancer is jumping.

Moving on to **Developpés**, we find an exercise which, as the name suggests, involves the slow unfolding of the working leg front or back to extend, with the foot well pointed, into an *arabesque*. Balance is vital in this exercise and though you will be helped here by the barre it is really preparing you for the exercises in the centre when you will have no support.

When you move on to the fast, sharp, beating movements of the feet called **Petits Battements** you will again be preparing yourself for the fast-moving beating steps you will do in the centre practice, especially steps such as the *entrechat*. Your working leg is moving from the knee down, with your thigh held steadily and, it now should go without saying, well turned out. A natural progression from this step will be the **Grands Battements**, the big beatings during which the whole leg will do a controlled swing from the hip socket. But never forget that, like every exercise, however high you swing the leg you must always be conscious of the movements which go into it; cleanly going through *tendu* to *glissée* and then up before reversing the sequence back to the starting position. Usually the swing up is clean and sharp, the

return slower and more controlled. The best description I have heard is that you should leave the floor as though it is red hot and return as though you remember it is! When you do the *grands battements* to the front and the side the body should be straight, but when you perform them to the back the body is allowed to tilt naturally forward a little so that the leg has a good height at the back.

We are now reaching the end of the barre and the best way to end is to do some stretching exercises which suit you, using the barre as support. While stretching and limbering up always remember the basic rules of posture, the way you hold your hips, your *ports de bras* and the way you hold your head.

After all this strenuous work at the barre your body should be ready for work in the centre of the studio, not surprisingly usually called centre work! Your muscles are warm and, if you have been wise in the way you have held the barre, you will have started to develop the balance which will be necessary for the exercises you are about to do. As you do these you will start to realize how the steps are slowly being put together to form a dance and stop being just classroom exercises. Soon you will have to stop concentrating on the way you *do* the steps and pay attention to the way you *perform* them and the musical quality they should have.

Centre work will start with the **Adage**, the slow section, which will teach you balance and co-ordination. You will also start to do *ports de bras* with both your arms now that you are free from the barre. Soon turns will be introduced, as well as small jumps and eventually the big jumps which you will see in the great classic pas de deux, for which you will also start to work with a partner. For girls there will be exercises to develop pointe work.

You will also start to work on a greater variety of positions of the body. Up to now exercises have been done either from the side or to the front, but you will learn *croisé, éffacé* and *écarté* as they are the most common. In *croisé* your working leg will cross the line of the supporting leg, but will be open in the *éffacé* position. You can see the difference in the accompanying illustrations. When you are in *écarté* your body will be at a diagonal angle to the audience with your working leg opened to second position.

The way the centre practice develops can vary from teacher to teacher, but the basic sequence will be the same and involve the following steps and positions. One of the earliest poses to be established in the classical ballet was the **Attitude** inspired by the statue of Mercury by Giovanni da Bologna. It is a very simple pose which consists of standing on one leg with the working leg raised behind the body and bent at the knee. As with so many steps we have already talked about there are variations in the different schools of teaching, but in general the knee should be higher than the foot, though even this rule which was once regarded as standard is now subject to change. Teachers in the West prefer to have the knee bent almost at right angles, while the Russian school prefers a wider angle which makes for a longer line. In all versions the raised knee is kept well behind the body. Your *ports de bras* can vary, but in general the basic one is to raise the same arm as the raised leg with the other held out to the side in second position. Hips must be kept square and the raised thigh should be as near as possible to parallel with the floor. In this position you can pirouette, be turned round in a circle on the spot by your partner, *promenade*, or balance on pointe as Aurora does during the Rose Adage of *The Sleeping Beauty*.

The various **Arabesques** you will perform require the same harmony of position as the *attitudes*. They too are performed by standing on one leg with your working leg raised as high as possible behind you, stretched to the full. You should keep your body in the same position as you raise your leg so that there is a natural line right through your body from finger tip to outstretched toe. The way you hold your arms in any of the *ports de bras* you use with the *arabesque* is very important, as any strain will spoil the overall effect and cause a harsh line. Part of the art of the *arabesque* is to find out the truly natural line of your body as you slowly raise your leg (from fifth position and not second) behind you, judging by instinct the amount of tilt you should allow your torso, to create the most beautiful effect. The only exception to this is when you deliberately allow your body to move forward to let the foot fly quite high in an **Arabesque**

Peter Schaufuss in a spectacular jump from the *Corsaire pas de deux*. ▶

Ib Anderson performing a *grande écarté* in a Bournonville ballet, *Dances from William Tell*.

Dinna Bjorn of the Royal Danish Ballet in a typical *attitude* jump which is often used in ballets by the great Danish choreographer August Bournonville.

Penchée such as you will see during the opening of the Kingdom of the Shades scene from *La Bayadère*.

Pirouettes must be the hardest step of a ballet class to describe in words. They form the group of turning steps which in turn will take their name from the position in which they are performed, turns in *attitude*, turns in *arabesque* or in second position for instance. The most basic pirouettes you will have learned will consist of a single complete turn of the body starting from second, fourth or fifth position. Your teacher will have progressed to a full turn through a quarter turn, then a half and then a three-quarter turn. Holding fifth position you will find the centre of balance of your body before doing a *demi-plié* to give you the push-off force to turn. From the *demi-plié* you will raise your working leg to a *sur le cou de pied* position as you rise onto *demi-pointe* and turn. Turning from fourth position will give you a stronger push off and will eventually be very useful for boys to perform their *pirouette à la seconde*. Just as you will find that some dancers have a natural spring, a natural ability to jump, so you will find that others have a natural ability to turn. If you are not one of these, work carefully at turns, but never throw your body around with too much force. It is still a wise rule to follow that in the world of classical ballet the quality of a step is more important than the quantity. Two perfectly executed turns are bound to be better than several done with inelegant force and quite possibly an untidy ending.

You will soon come to the part of centre work which is made up of small jumps, **Petit Allegro**, designed to warm you up for the big jumps which will come later. They are not virtuoso jumps and are all done from two legs, landing on two legs. All the jumps work through the foot to help build elegance and control, pressing into the ground as you leave, with the toe the last to leave the ground. This will mean that your instep is fully stretched. Variations include the **soubresauté** which is a quick jump up from fifth position through a *demi-plié* returning back to the ground in fifth. While you are up in the air only the front foot should be visible to someone watching you from directly in front. **Changements** are a development from the *soubresauté* as your feet will change position while in the air, slowly taking you towards the *entrechat*. A variation on a simple *changement*, mostly performed by girls is the **pas de chat**, literally meaning jumping like a cat. It is a jump to the side with the leading leg bending in the air on the way up while the following leg does the same on the downward movement. The effect at the middle point of the movement if it could be held still for a moment would look a little like a *demi-plié* in the air. As you might expect this step appears in the variation for the White Cat in the wedding celebrations in *The Sleeping Beauty*. This is, in a way, a travelling jump, just like **Brisé Volé** which will be mostly performed by boys in such variations as the Bluebird. It is a travelling step with a beat included in the sequence, the beat being performed to the front and to the back alternatively as the dancer crosses the floor. This is very much a virtuoso step which will only come in advanced training. Another special step, but one which gains its effect by elegance as much as by excitement, is the **Temps de Poisson** which is a high jump as you might imagine a fish doing if, like a salmon, it jumped out of the water. To do it beautifully your body would arch backwards while you are in the air, with your arms held high in fifth position. The whole movement up in the air has to look sleek and elegant with no strain in the body at all. The one major mistake often made is to bend the knees in order to try to create a greater arc. It always looks terrible! Moving on to the beaten steps in the centre, **Batterie**, you will have reached the *entrechats* and *cabrioles* as well as the *brisés* we have already mentioned in one form. An **Entrechat** involves you jumping straight up and down with a varying number of changes of the position of the feet from which the *entrechat* takes its name. From the *changement* you have already performed you will progress to **Entrechat trois**, **Entrechat quatre**, **Entrechat cinq**, **Entrechat six** and so on, until you progress to **Entrechat douze** which will earn you a place in the Guinness Book of Records! You will rarely be expected to perform more than *entrechat six* in any of the classic variations. The basic *entrechat* which would be the *entrechat deux* is usually referred to as a **royal** for which you start from fifth position, with the correct *ports de bras*, and jump into the air from a smooth *demi-plié*. For an *entrechat quatre* you start with the right foot in front and while in the air move the left to the front, on the way down changing back to right front again landing as you started. *Entrechat six* is a progression so that the extra change in the air means you end with the opposite foot in front. Odd numbered *entrechat* are the same except you will land on one foot.

Having worked so far you reach the **Jetés**, the big exciting jumps. No words can explain how they should work, other than to say that however exciting and abandoned they look to the audience they should be as carefully controlled as any other step, cutting cleanly through the air, with well-held *ports de bras*, and good **ballon**, the light bouncing quality every dancer should have. Equally exciting steps, used in the virtuoso pas de deux are the **Fouettés** for the girls and **Tours en l'Air** for the boys, although no

one step is ever only performed by one or the other. The fast whipping turns of the ballerina are always show-stoppers. The simplest *fouettés* start from a single *pirouette* from fifth position to give momentum, the working leg as it is in front being brought into sharp *retiré* as you turn, the whole body, including the head, turning (this is when you find your 'spot') and back right round to the front. A *tour en l'air* is exactly what it sounds like, one or more complete revolutions of the body up in the air. Just as 32 single *fouettés* were once regarded as special for the ballerina but now she should include doubles, so triple *tours en l'air* can be expected of the boy, though they have to be done so fast that you can barely work out that they have been done! As boys continue with special virtuoso steps, the girls will do exercises on pointe. Though some professional dancers are happy to do a whole class on pointe, while still a student, the amount of pointe work must be carefully judged by your teacher.

After all the exercises apart, some days boys and girls will be brought together for **double work**, indeed will probably have a whole period set aside for it. The boy must learn to show off his ballerina to best advantage; to make her feel secure and confident while at the same time keeping a good presence for himself as he is part of the performance and not just a 'porter' in the worst sense of the word. He must also learn to harmonize his movements with those of the ballerina so that his *ports de bras* complement hers to make a complete picture. Only by continual practice can this, just like your basic technique, become truly instinctive.

Mary Jago and Peter Schaufuss in *La Bayadère*.

Once you, and your parents, have decided that you really want to take up dance as a career, there is a very good chance that you will go to a boarding school, though if you are lucky you might live near a good school which takes day pupils. If you are particularly lucky, and talented, you might try to gain entry to the Royal Ballet School. If you succeed, you will start in the Junior School and this is what life is like on a typical day . . .

At the Royal Ballet School

The day at White Lodge begins at 7.15 a.m. with the ring of the rising bell. Just as at ordinary boarding schools some children spring eagerly from their beds while others linger. But ordinary this school is not, for Richmond Park's White Lodge (once the hunting lodge of King George V) is the home of The Royal Ballet Lower School, where the cream of young British ballet students go to train.

Hundreds of youngsters apply each year for entry to the school, but from them only about 20 11-year olds are selected for the first year. Some 12-year olds join in the second year, and a few 13-year olds in the third. Thirteen, though, is late to start serious ballet training.

Successful entrants have been carefully chosen from preliminary and then final auditions, where a team of experts has assessed not just their dance ability, but also musicality and physical suitability. Bodies have to be suitably proportioned, and this is difficult to assess given that children are changing physically all the time. Tests can determine eventual height to within an inch and a half, but it is hard to predict whether the child will fill out excessively in adolescence. Bone structure, as an indicator of ultimate shape, reveals the frames that will remain slender and identifies those that will grow stocky. Once all the tests have been passed, and a child's 'skeleton' is approved by the ballet staff, an orthopaedic examination follows to check that there are no hidden abnormalities in bones and muscles.

Children are *never* taken into the school because their mothers think it would be glamorous for them to have a stage career. The training is far too rigorous for anyone who is less than totally committed, and White Lodge pupils share a passion for ballet. The goal is graduation into The Royal Ballet or the Sadler's Wells Royal Ballet. Ambitions are focused on this throughout their five years at the Lower School and their final years at the Upper School in London's Barons Court.

Today, as on every working day, the girls and boys arrive from their separate wings for breakfast at 8.15 a.m. They seem like ordinary children as they fill the dining room with chatter, but they do move unconsciously well and there are no slouchers among them. Also it is perhaps unusual to see girls who, without exception, have long hair.

Once breakfast is over there is a rush of activity, with everyone scampering off to collect books or shoes in preparation for the day's work. In the entrance hall there is a life-sized sculpture of Margot Fonteyn, and six small girls pass it on their way to get their written work from their dormitory. Instead of walking they execute neat coupés chassés (travelling steps in which the weight transfers from foot to foot), and as they pass the statue each one makes a swift turn, as if in homage to The Royal Ballet's Prima Ballerina Assoluta. It is a telling moment.

The fifth formers have made straight for the ballet studios, using all the time available to warm up and stretch their limbs. At 8.45 a.m. the girls' teacher, Nancy Kilgour, sets the exercise for pliés, and the familiar pattern of the daily class begins.

Dancers are not made overnight, they evolve from years and years of work, and so training at the school is slow and careful. It follows traditions built up since Louis XIV's time, with particular emphasis on the British style developed by the founder of The Royal Ballet schools and companies, Ninette de Valois, and by its first choreographer, Frederick Ashton. But these traditions are open to new ideas and scientific discoveries, as well as other international styles of schools of dance.

Teacher and pupils work together for an entire year, and so Mrs. Kilgour knows the measure of each one of her charges' skills and shortcomings, sensing when to galvanize with hard criticism or when to encourage with praise. As the class proceeds she urges, 'Dance dynamically with the music. Kirov

dancers would put more energy, more excitement into the step.' By making her pupils think of the height of a Russian arabesque their movements visibly expand.

Yesterday as a treat the fifth-form girls were taken to the Upper School to watch students two or three years ahead of them in the Graduate Girls class. This is the top class, from which dancers may be drawn at any time into one of the two companies. This term the girls were being taught by an international guest, Mona Vangsaae, once a well-known Danish dancer and now a revered teacher and coach. There is added excitement among both participants and spectators, for the experience she brings to her work and because her own schooling is part of an unbroken line from the greatest of all Danish choreographers and teachers, August Bournonville. His work in the 19th century is still important today, indeed Miss Vangsaae is staging *Konservatoriet*, one of his ballets, for The Royal Ballet.

Mona Vangsaae, who created the role of Juliet in
Sir Frederick Ashton's *Romeo and Juliet* teaching
at The Royal Ballet School.

Back at White Lodge today, however, the fifth-form boys' class takes place separately at the same time as the girls'. While ballet has long been a popular career for girls, only in recent years has it begun to attract large numbers of boys, making entry to the school increasingly competitive. Of the 120 pupils, roughly a third are boys. Their time-table is similar to the girls', except that regular gymnastics and weight-lifting sessions help to give them added muscular strength.

After their hour and a half class, and a short break, the fifth formers return to their separate studios for concentrated work on particular areas of study. Today the girls do pointe work for an hour, while the boys turn their attention to elevation and to improving their jumps.

Meanwhile everyone else is at work in the educational wing, and here girls and boys work together. Studies include the usual range of subjects taught at school, though without a wide specialist choice. Dancers are not expected to shine academically, but they do need a lively intelligence. It is no coincidence that the most successful are often also the brightest at school work! The fifth formers' school day is particularly hard, for as soon as they arrive at their desks they have to devote their full attention to the approaching exams.

With the younger pupils, two 40-minute lessons are followed by a break for orange juice and biscuits, and then Form I have French. The 11-year olds have only been at the school for a few weeks, and standards are mixed. But classes are small, giving the teacher a chance to attend to everyone's individual abilities. The bright ones among them raise their hands, eager to give the required French translation for a short English sentence. One little boy, exasperated because he gets the answer wrong, apologizes: 'Sorry Mrs. Vlasto, I didn't put my brain in today!'

In the laboratory Form II are having a human biology lesson and analyzing blood. The brave ones prick their fingers, squeezing a drop or two of their own onto a glass slide under the microscope. Suddenly there is a chorus of worried voices from the group clustered round the central table; 'Please Mrs. Keene, Alison hasn't got any cells'. Mrs. Keene hurries to the microscope and allays fears by proving that in fact Alison has perfectly normal cells.

In other classrooms groups are busy with English and geography lessons, but Form IV has moved back to the main wing for their ballet class. The children come into contact with an unusually large number of teachers, because there are two sets of staff; one for vocational and one for educational lessons. This means that fees are high, but White Lodge parents pay only a proportion (according to income) of the total cost, the remainder being contributed by government funds. In most other European countries and in Russia, specialist training is paid for entirely by the state, while in America, at the School of American Ballet for example, a committee raises funds to cover the student's costs. But no British child who appears to have real talent is ever refused training for lack of funds.

All day long there are music lessons to be fitted in. Nearly all pupils learn to play an instrument, and not surprisingly piano is the most popular. An entire basement corridor opens out into cell-like piano rooms, and some of the dormitories also have pianos

in them. Out of working hours these can give great entertainment.

Lunch is eaten in shifts. The food is quite simple, and today it is sausages, potatoes and baked beans, a glass of milk, and jelly to follow. Everyone eats sensibly, fuelling themselves for the afternoon classes. Choosey eaters are frowned on, and there are no special diets, except for religious or health reasons.

Three girls come running along the corridor, impatient to join the queue, but they bump straight into the senior ballet mistress. Miss Wadsworth sends them back to walk down the corridor with decorum. Though crestfallen they obey without a murmur, for discipline is an essential quality in a dancer.

After lunch it is the turn of the middle and junior pupils (in sequence according to years) to have their ballet classes. In the studio all is quiet and orderly. The children are happiest in their ballet classes, generally preferring hard work to the idleness of holidays, though once they have settled into White Lodge they will find things to complain about in the way of all healthy youngsters!

Form III boys are a talented bunch, working with an almost military precision just like a well-drilled regiment. 'Boys are much easier to teach than girls', observes their teacher Richard Glasstone, 'they don't try and confuse their movement with fancy steps'. Even so no teacher makes predictions for the future; there are too many pitfalls.

Although all the children have proved their worth at the two entry auditions, it is made clear that they are on trial throughout their training. In February each year they are normally assessed, and those who do not match up to the school's high standards, or whose physical development is unsatisfactory (too fat, too thin, too tall, too short or whatever) are asked to leave at the end of the summer term. Everyone accepts the necessity of weeding out, but no child wants to leave.

Even those who progress satisfactorily through White Lodge, and then move on for two or three further years to the Upper School, may still not make the grade by graduation time. They may not grow into dancers who look like Royal Ballet candidates (and a company's style and look, with dancers conforming to a certain type and shape, is all-important), or they may be unlucky enough to be members of a vintage year in which talented students outnumber company vacancies. In this case they will be advised to audition for other British or European companies.

Since ballet is dependent on perfect physical fitness, there is always the possibility that a serious injury could ruin a promising future, so it is impressed on all the children that they must keep an open mind about other careers.

No such worries are troubling Form II, who are by now engrossed in their art class, and in making Christmas decorations. The girls gather admiringly round one boy's desk very impressed with his painting. Away from the group, another concentrates on finishing his model, oblivious to any distraction. Despite the art class's enthusiasm, when the bell goes they all rush eagerly to the ballet studio.

Mr. Glasstone gives 12-year olds a tough class. 'Children are capable of far more than adults give them credit for,' he insists. As if in acknowledgement of his words the boys strive harder to point their feet, deepen their demi-pliés and jump higher.

At 3.05 p.m., the first years arrive for class. The girls' teacher is Christine Beckley who, like many of the ballet staff, is a former member of The Royal Ballet, a fact that gives the pupils a privileged proximity to the profession.

Despite their youth the little girls are immaculately groomed. From the start they have been instructed in ways of fixing their hair so that there are no untidy whisps, and tying the ribbons on their shoes so that no 'pig's ears' escape.

Miss Beckley teaches with a mixture of kindness and simulated fierceness, to which they respond in good part. They are busily preparing their Demonstration Class, which they have to show to the Ballet Principal, Barbara Fewster, and all the teachers the following week; already their lines are as uniform as a first-rate corps de ballet.

Normally school finishes for everyone at 4.20 p.m., but today is special for eight 11- and 12-year-old girls and boys, since they have a small part in the evening performance of *Konservatoriet*.

They clamber into the school's mini-bus for the drive to the Royal Opera House at Covent garden, with Miss Wadsworth and a matron. The children have to be carefully supervised, and the law demands that every child appearing on stage must have a special licence as a safeguard against exploitation. No Royal Ballet School Child would come up against this problem, for the school is very strict about allowing its pupils to appear in public. Apart from rare appearances when children are needed in a repertory ballet, they only go on stage at the annual Covent Garden performance (since this is a school, not a professional, performance no licence is needed). While other vocational schools may show their pupils in complicated, challenging ballets, The Royal Ballet Lower School sensibly only lets its children perform Folk Dances from England, Ireland, Scotland and Wales. These are relatively simple, but their uniform skill makes them a popular highlight of the performance (following which the Upper School students present ballet from the companies' repertory). The following week, during a brief season at Sadler's Wells Theatre, some of the 13- to 15-year-olds may also dance in a specially created short work, but the emphasis is mainly on the work of the Upper School.

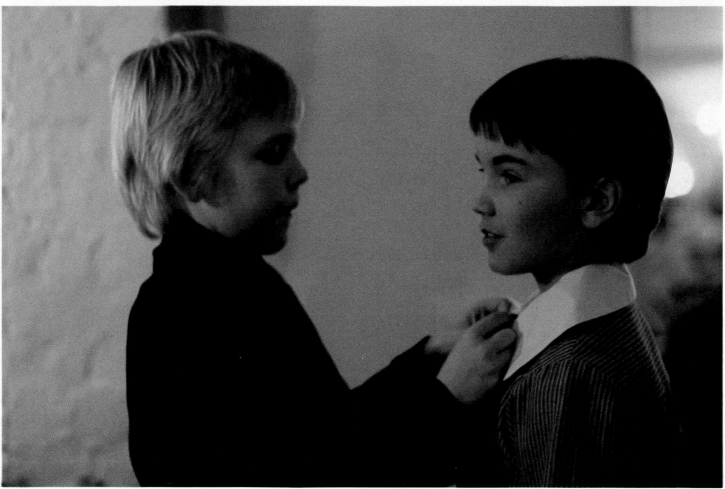

At 5.30 p.m. the mini-bus reaches the stage door, and as the children cross the door to enter Covent Garden's magical world the doorman's warm smile greets them. Although only eight are needed in the performance, six extras go in case of injury or illness. They all go down to the canteen for supper, which everyone looks on as a big treat and a welcome relief from school food. Afterwards Miss Wadsworth leads them through a maze of corridors to their dressing rooms, bags are unpacked, and preparations for the performance begin.

They wear track suits over their leotards and tights, and as they start changing they stretch themselves in a few warm-up exercises. The hairdresser comes in to fix ringlets of curls around the girls' hair, and Miss Wadsworth starts applying a light make-up on the evening's cast. The understudies pull out their

school books, for they are expected to fit in as much of their regular hour of prep (homework) as possible. They will gladly jump up and lend a helping hand with the dressing when it seems necessary.

While the rest of their classmates are enjoying free time at White Lodge, and perhaps working on a short piece of choreography, playing table tennis, or watching television, the dressing room is abuzz with chatter and small children busily checking that every last detail of their costume is in order.

When a voice over the loud-speaker system running from stage to dressing room calls 'five minutes ladies and gentlemen' they are taken up to the stage. There is time for a brief grouping on stage, and a quick think about the steps before they are ushered to the sides (wings). The house lights dim, there is a hush and the overture begins. The dancers on stage go into their opening sequence, and then it is the children's turn to run into line to present a few simple steps and jumps. Their choreography is not unlike the centre practice exercises that they do every day in class, but in their rehearsals Miss Vangsaae has paid close attention to Bournonville's style. They were told to imagine that they held flowers between their fingers, but not too tightly or they would be crushed to death.

Tonight's principals are Rudolf Nureyev, Antoinette Sibley and Merle Park, and when the children's dance is over and they have returned to the wings, they crane their necks to catch a glimpse of Miss Park. For today it has been announced that she will succeed James Monahan as Director of the school from September 1983.

Afterwards the children make their bows, then hurry back to the dressing rooms, remove costume and make-up, put on track suits, file back along the corridors, say good-night to the stage doorman and climb back into the mini-bus.

They reach White Lodge soon after 9.00 p.m., glowing with excitement, and longing to tell their friends about the performance, particularly about how wonderful Miss Park was. After sandwiches and hot drinks they are hustled off to bed, soon the lights are out and everyone sleeps.

Tomorrow will be just another ordinary working day. Except life at White Lodge is never really ordinary.

Like any trade or profession dancers have to look after what they use; their shoes, practice clothes and, most importantly, their bodies. Out of the many things needed to cope with a dancing life here are a few . . .

Hints for the Young Dancer

What to wear

Ballet stockists sell all sorts of glamorous clothes for dance. However many schools insist on a uniform, so check before you buy. If the choice is left to you, it is sometimes difficult to know where to start. Simplicity is often the best policy, because it is important to look neat and uncluttered. Try to buy garments that are a good quality and made to last because they will get a lot of wear.

Once girls and boys stop wearing party clothes to baby ballet classes, girls generally wear leotards, and boys a tee-shirt or singlet and shorts. From about 11 girls look most suitable in black or pink tights and a black leotard with three-quarter length sleeves. Boys are best in black tights (with a dance belt underneath) and a white tee-shirt. To start with be careful about investing in layers of woollen garments because they can prevent the teacher from spotting early faults and weaknesses. Extra accessories can be indulged in when the body is beginning to acquire a trained look, when all-over tights and more vivid colours are worn.

Shoes

Simple flat ballet shoes should be chosen with care to fit the feet, and not with room for growth. Pink leather is the traditional colour for girls, and black for boys. They are fastened with elastic sewn on either side. To determine where to position the elastic, press the heel forwards pushing inwards from the centre: the diagonals that appear on either side give the sewing line. Sometimes girls prefer to have ribbons on their shoes. These should be half-an-inch wide and you will find advice on sewing them under the Pointe Shoes section which follows.

Pointe Shoes

Pointe shoes should fit like a second skin, but because no two people's feet are alike it may take time, effort and experiment to find the most suitable size and make. The shoes need to be bought through one of the specialist manufacturers (details can be found through advertisements in the dance magazines) under the eye of a properly qualified assistant. Roughly half a dozen firms have long-established reputations, and it may be necessary to visit several,

even having shoes specially made for a small fee, before finding the most suitable style. Fit is not just a matter of testing the length and width of the foot, but of taking other factors into account such as the length of heel and wamp (the block). A dancer with a high instep, for example, requires support from a high wamp, whereas a dancer without much instep will probably need a low wamp to help give the illusion of a better arched foot.

Traditionally pink satin shoes are the most popular. Leather shoes, especially in black, might seem more practical, but they do not look so good and are seldom worn.

Preparation

Pointe shoes take a lot of looking after. Initially, you have to decide which shoe goes best on which foot, then the sewing, breaking in, hardening, and cleaning are fun because they seem so professional. Later they become nothing more than a necessary chore, but a vital one because untidy, dirty shoes in performances are an immediate sign of insufficient care in preparation.

Ribbons

Ribbons (three-quarters of an inch wide and purchased with the shoes) are the first essential. They must be sewn very securely. A ribbon coming unattached from the shoe is unthinkable! To find the correct positioning, take the heel of the shoe and push it forward from the centre: the diagonals that appear on either side give the line for the back edge of the ribbon. Cut the ribbons into four even lengths, take one of these, measure about one and a quarter inches and fold the end back about a third of the way. Next place it along one diagonal and hem neatly down the back edge, continue hemming across the fold, up the other side and along the outside top edge of the shoe (taking care not to catch the drawstring). It is a good idea to stitch back across the top for extra security before fastening off carefully and pulling out the final stitch from between the satin and the canvas lining.

The entire operation (which soon becomes automatic) is of course repeated on the opposite side, and then on the other shoe.

Once the shoes have worn out and are fit only for the dustbin, the ribbons should be unpicked, washed, and sewn onto another pair.

Darning

Most students darn the toes, to preserve the satin and prevent jagged tears that give the shoes a mis-shapen look. There are many different ways of going about this including making and sewing on little crochet caps which soon come unstitched from the shoes. The best equipment is often carpet thread and a curved needle about one and a half inches long. You darn the shoe by making a line from the end of the sole and around the edge of the pointe, then stretching the thread across from side to side and subsequently weaving it in and out in the opposite direction and every so often catching the satin into the stitch. Warning! Use a thimble because this is tough sewing.

The ribbons if correctly positioned should be all that is needed to keep the shoe secured, though there is an increasing (and unattractive) tendency to sew elastic on either side of the shoe and loop it over the foot. If elastic is really necessary it should be lined up with the heel, or stitched ribbons. It should not be too thick and should be the same colour as the tights to make it as inconspicuous as possible.

Preservation

Some dancers pour a little liquid shellac inside the shoes to harden and thus lengthen their lives from the start. Shellac is a brown substance usually available from an ironmonger's shop, and if used care should be taken to apply a very small amount, and to swirl it inside the toe – but gently otherwise it will seep through and ruin the look of the satin. It should be left to dry for about 12 hours.

Alternatively shellac may be applied after the shoes have softened through use. But a simple trick like resting used shoes may make them seem harder after a few days.

Wearing

Once the shoes are prepared, the next hurdle is wearing them. When first put on they will probably seem uncomfortable and unwieldy. But persevere!

The drawstrings threaded through the top of each shoe should be dealt with first. They need to be pulled up when the shoe is on so that it feels comfortably secure, then tied into a small bow and tucked away out of sight in the space between shoe and foot.

To tie the ribbon on the right foot, pull the left ribbon over the front of the ankle and cross the right on top of it. Take both round to the back of the ankle, transfer to the opposite hands and, keeping the same direction bring ribbons round to the front again and cross neatly on the ankle one on top of the other.

This time take the left side three-quarter way round the ankle to meet the right one just above the bone and tie the two into a knot (preferably a reef). The ribbons should now be firm but not so tight that they stop the blood circulating. Cut the ends so that just over an inch extends from the knot, and tuck them (the thin handle of a long comb may help) under the top of the ribbon until they disappear completely.

Repeat the process on the other foot, ensuring that the outside ribbon makes its first cross on top of the inside one.

Breaking in

Breaking in is just a matter of the feet and shoes getting used to one another. Experienced students may simply take a few steps round the studio on demi-pointe to soften the shoe backs, step up on pointe a couple of times and rise into a relevé or two. They are then ready to respond to whatever exercises are set.

The young student must only work on pointe under the watchful eye of a teacher, because serious injuries can result from inexperience. Incidentally, exercises on pointe are usually done towards the end of class when the body and limbs are thoroughly warmed up.

Professional dancers whose feet and ankles have strengthened through years of hard work often prefer to have really pliable shoes for performances. They treat them mercilessly, banging them against concrete floors, thrusting them between the hinges of a door which they then swing backwards and forwards, even ripping out the small, strong inner sole which is hidden away under the inner cardboard sole. Students, as a rule, need harder shoes and should not attempt such tricks, though it is quite a good idea to remove the inner sole when shoes are no longer strong enough for pointe work and are turned into 'flatties' for regular classwork.

Presentation of the satin

Ballet companies take pride in creating a uniformly groomed effect, and because the shade of pink in the shoes varies between manufacturers, the dancers often sponge them all over with a theatrical make-up base. This ensures that all shoes have the same matt pink, and it also hides dirty smudges (although it takes away the lovely sheen).

It would be silly for students to go to the trouble and expense of making-up shoes. Cleaning fluids such as Beaucaire, applied with cotton wool, may help remove surface stains, but when it is essential to preserve the shoes' newness for an end of term show or an exam, a useful trick is to cut the toe and heel out of an old pair of socks and wear these over the shoes.

Rosin

A word of caution, socks may be slippery and rosin may be needed. Rosin is a white powdery substance which is kept in a shallow wooden box in a corner of most studios to help prevent slipping. It is vital to use it on highly polished floors, but not on those which already provide an adequate grip. Dancers, however, are creatures of habit and drift towards the rosin box with the compulsion of a nervous twitch – for just standing in it and coating the soles and pointes of their shoes with rosin inspires confidence. It can have an adverse effect when, for example, they need to do a fast pirouette. The rosin and the floor between them conspire to give too tight a hold!

The rosin box at the ready under the table in the wings.

Pain

Try not to think too much about the formation of blisters, bunions and blood when you go on pointe, just remember that you are part of a long tradition of dancers suffering for their art. Lambswool between the toes may help ease some of the pain caused as the foot rubs against the shoe. Keep a plaster handy for patching up later. Do not go looking for problems because they do not afflict everyone.

Injuries

Injuries for the dancer, as for the athlete, are a hazard. If the rules are followed they should not happen, but when they do, it is often because a dancer is tired and has pushed him or herself into a sudden, careless movement. They damage morale not just on account of the immediate pain, but for the frustration of having an exceptionally healthy body which is then unable to work fully.

If you are injured turn the problem around and use it positively! Watch the class, observe where your fellow students go wrong and resolve to do better when you return. If it is your ankle that is hurt, lie on your back and do stretching and strengthening exercises through gentle raising, pulling and slow lowering of the legs. Then lie on your front and raise legs and stretched arms, separately and together, holding them for an increasing number of counts. Floor exercises can be extremely beneficial, strengthening weak muscles while ensuring that the body is evenly placed.

But all injuries must be looked after carefully and may need professional advice. Advice takes many forms, some more suited to dance than others. It is possible to go to a doctor with a strained leg muscle three days before the premiere of a show. He may prescribe three weeks in bed to cure it. You may tell him that this is impossible – at which point he may get angry and ask you what is the point of going to see him if you will not take his advice. You may then visit an osteopath and be cured within minutes! As you can see it may be necessary to take an injury to a practitioner of what is termed 'fringe' medicine. Some doctors do not recognize the work they do, and certainly there are still some people working in this field who give them reason to be suspicious, but in general osteopaths and independent physiotherapists do excellent work. The best way to locate one is by word of mouth, or you could ask a nearby football club or sports centre. If you have no choice but to find someone from the telephone directory ask for his or her credentials. Anyone registered with the British School of Osteopathy for example, should be quite safe and there are similar recognized organizations around the world.

Fringe medicine can be expensive, but if it avoids absence from classes that have already been paid for it may be a saving in the long run.

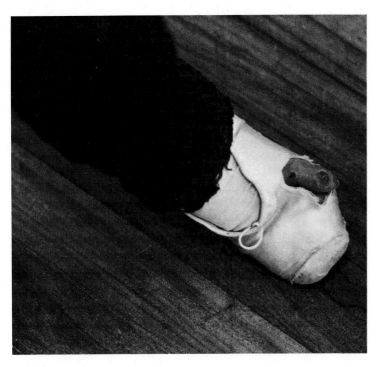
The unglamorous side of dance: a pointe shoe cut to fit a damaged toe.

Knitting

A good way of watching television constructively is to knit! When you're going to ballet classes you'll probably want woollies, tights, leg warmers or crossovers, so buy a pattern, some knitting needles and wool, and get going. If knitting is not your strong point, try something more modest such as ankle warmers. If you're more confident, it is possible to knit leg warmers without a pattern. Use ribbing for the ankle, calculating the number of stitches per inch and then measuring accordingly to find the total number that you need. Keep the pattern going for about two and a half inches, then change to stocking stitch and knit up the leg, increasing the stitches at regular intervals (say every inch). Keep a note of the mathematics so that you can copy them for the second leg. After you have cast off (loosely), thread narrow elastic round the top of the warmer, so that it stays in position. Alternatively, invent, or use a tested rib stitch the whole way.

While you're knitting sit on the floor with your back straight and find a useful stretching position. You might, for example, put the soles of your feet together and leave the knees to see whether gravity will pull them gradually to the floor! Or if you've got plenty of space to yourself you could sit with your legs in as wide a second position (to the side) as you can manage. Even sitting cross legged with your back supported by a straight wall is beneficial. But do not do anything silly that hurts, do not jerk your limbs or overstretch, and do check with your teacher to ensure that your sitting positions are safe.

Diet and a word of caution

All dancers are dissatisfied with their figures – they are too fat or too thin, their legs are too short, their arms are too long, their faces lack high cheekbones and so on. Training can help some, but not all of these defects. Outside the classroom diet plays a vital part, but it is equally vital not to be extreme in your eating habits and to eat a sensible well-balanced diet, because dancers are useless without health and stamina. Some people starve themselves for days and then have secret binges because they cannot stand the hunger pangs any more, or they starve themselves for so long that they get a disease called *anorexia nervosa* which means they cannot eat and may end up in hospital. In both cases the end results interfere seriously with career prospects.

In all eating patterns there should be a sensible amount of protein, vitamin, fat and carbohydrate. Eat plenty of salads and raw fruit, and good, fresh, lightly-cooked vegetables, meat, cheese and milk, though it is wise not to eat too many dairy products because they are fattening if eaten in excess. Muesli, wholemeal bread, brown rice, pulses and bean sprouts are also firm favourites with dancers. Pulses such as dried beans and peas are good because they are much less expensive than meat, and just as nutritious. Of all the diet books, Audrey Eyton's *The F Plan Diet* (Penguin) can help you feel healthy and slim without the usual agonies of deprivation and/or high expenditure.

How to Improve the Shining Hours

When you have a bit of spare time find out about ballet history and dancers' lives and extend your understanding of ballet. If your library is not well stocked, talk the assistants into ordering more dance books. Find out from your newsagent which dance magazines are available (*Dance and Dancers* and *Dancing Times* in Britain, *Ballet News* and *Dance Magazine* in the United States, for example), and place a regular order or ask for a subscription for your next birthday. Ask for presents of book tokens and buy ballet books from your local bookshop. Study the pictures because they help to give you an understanding of what you are working for in class. Spend weekends with a friend sticking pictures from newspapers and other magazines into a scrapbook. Save your pocket money for ballet tickets; remembering that visits to concerts, opera, theatre, art galleries or museums can enhance your appreciation.

Do not get so involved with your ballet school that you never look beyond its four walls. Go to as many ballet performances as you and your parents can afford. Watching everyone from stars to corps de ballet will be a lesson in itself; a more enjoyable lesson, perhaps, than your daily class!

When a young dancer graduates from school their thoughts naturally turn to finding a job. For the top students of a school such as the Royal Ballet School this is no problem as they will already know if they are going to become members of the Royal Ballet. For the others there will be letters to write and auditions to attend. But for all working dancers it is surprising how similar you will find the . . .

Dancer's Day

After the years of hard work in a ballet school the aim of every young dancer who wishes to make a professional career is to join a ballet company; the more important the better. For dancers in America to join the New York City Ballet or American Ballet Theater is their great ambition. Danish dancers will graduate into their own Royal Danish Ballet, just as the cream of the students at the Paris Opera will have their sights on becoming an *etoile*, a star, of their company. In Britain, the few top students of the Royal Ballet School can hope for a place in the Royal Ballet, based either in the Royal Opera House or at Sadler's Wells Theatre. Of course, there are always exceptions. Some young students might find life in a great company very restrictive and prefer to seek out a smaller company, perhaps one which will give them a greater chance to take part in new ballets or to work with a particular choreographer. After years learning the classical technique some find that their natural outlet might be in a modern dance company; others may go straight into theatre dance in cabaret or a musical. But whichever company, great or small, in whichever country, much of their daily life will be the same.

The day starts with class. No matter how great the ballerina, how temperamental the star, they will almost without exception join the lowliest corps de ballet member in the classroom to start the day. Artists who seemed so perfect on the stage the night before, who received tumultous applause and perhaps a shower of flowers, once again become students in simple practice clothes (or not-so-simple in these days of fantastic knitted leg-warmers and the variety of printed tee-shirts) ready to perform the exercises given at the barre and in the centre by an experienced teacher. Class may vary in length for the professional dancer depending on the amount of time available on the schedule, as time also has to be found for rehearsals, costume fittings and all the other activities which lead up to a performance.

Dancers have their trade union just like any other workers and the union will have negotiated on their behalf not only their pay, but also the conditions of work. The total number of hours permitted each day will have to include all activities, which means that on the day of a performance there is not time for everything. In Britain and America, for example, the hours are generally longer than in a state opera house such as in Sweden where the regulations are so strict that on a performance day there is barely time for a class as well as the evening show. Even the working temperature can be taken into account and rehearsals have been cancelled, as well as performances, if it was a degree or so lower than the agreed figure. This is not because the dancers are difficult. It is simply that injuries can happen so much easier if the body is subjected to low or frequently changing temperatures.

After the hard work of class it is possible, though unlikely, that a dancer can be free until the evening performance, especially if they are not in some new ballet which is being rehearsed or are not called for a rehearsal of something they have danced many times. It is much more likely that after studying the Call Board on which the day's activities are listed you will hear lots of groans as dancers realize that they have to wait around the theatre all day in order to have a few rehearsals scattered throughout the day.

Derek Rencher, famous for his fine acting in roles such as the evil magician in *The Firebird*, joins other boys of the Royal Ballet in an exercise during the morning class.

Sometimes to suit the timetable or because studio space is limited the class can take place in the elegant surroundings of the Crush Bar at the Royal Opera House.

Often it is not worth the bother (and risk) of dressing and leaving the theatre for a short time. This only makes it necessary to warm the body up again with additional exercises on their return – or risk injury and strain. The sight of groups of dancers sitting on the floor waiting while another rehearsal takes place is common in a theatre. But then, dancers never seem to tire of watching and learning.

If a new production is in preparation or there is a new cast there will be costume fittings to attend and very boring they can be for the dancer. Standing like a a tailor's dummy while costumes are pinned or stitched, doing a few movements to make sure they give enough freedom for dance or just standing while a designer actually paints a pattern onto some body tights, is not an amusing occupation. Hair styles have to be practised. Not only to see what they look like or how a new head-dress will fit, but also to

see how secure they can be made to avoid them flying off during some strenuous dancing. Even so, it is still a common sight to see pieces of jewellery flying across the stage or hair slowly coming undone. This can be an especially tricky problem in a full-length ballet such as *Swan Lake* when the girls of the corps de ballet, in particular, may have to have 'peasant' hair styles in the first act, perhaps with flowers entwined. They will then have only 15 minutes to change into a severe classical style with feathers for the second 'white' act as few companies are large enough to have a separate corps of swans. Then they must rush to change from swan into one of the character dancers of the third 'black' act. If this was not enough, some may well have to do the transformation into swan yet again for the fourth act. They must also think of make-up, costume and shoes at the same time.

Some of the endless hours of waiting during rehearsals can be taken up sewing shoes or doing very personal stretching exercises.

A costume parade in the Royal Opera Crush Bar for Kenneth MacMillan's *Gloria*. Monica Mason and Julian Hoskings have their headwear adjusted while MacMillan looks on in the background. ▶

When it comes to rehearsal time the work generally falls into three types; creating a new ballet with a choreographer, rehearsing a new individual role or the routine rehearsal of a basic ballet to keep it up to standard. Of these, the first is the most stimulating, the second excellent for the person concerned, but the third can be very tedious indeed. A dancer can contribute so much when working with many of the major choreographers. A few know precisely what they want before they come to the rehearsal and then show the dancer exactly what to do. Others rely heavily on the dancer and will ask for suggestions about how to develop movements or add some special twist. How many times have I seen a dancer make a mistake, slip out of the position the choreographer has arranged, and then heard 'Let's keep that in'. Working on a new role for themselves most dancers have little problem with concentration, especially since it may be an important step up in their career. Working on routine corps de ballet movements only occasionally needs great powers of concentration and often the tedium can only be relieved by jokes

Merle Park and David Wall rehearsing with David Bintley, one of the Royal Ballet's brightest young choreographers.

A company rehearsal on stage.

Marguerite Porter being rehearsed in the Mad Scene of *Giselle* by Gerd Larsen.

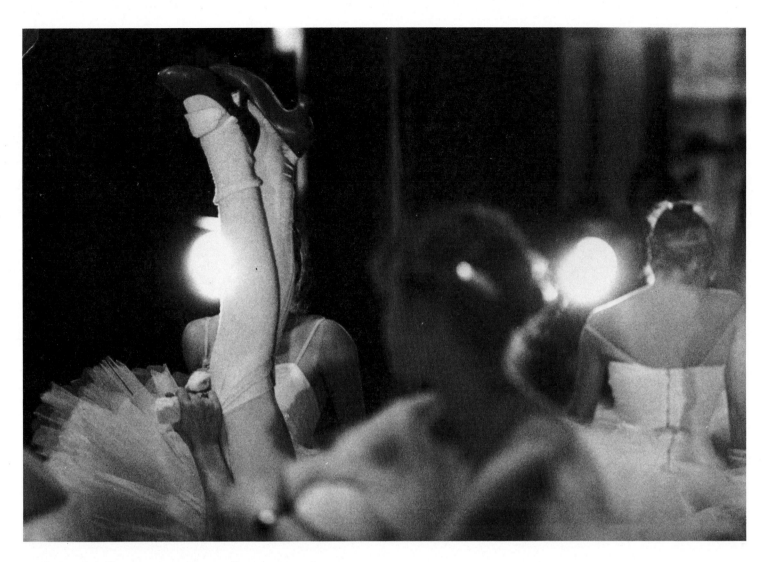

and pranks. Dancers are naturally very good at mimicking each other which can so often relieve the tension of a tricky situation.

When you look at photographs of dancers in class, dancers sitting in studios during rehearsals, dancers talking dance in the green room or canteen you realize how much time they spend with each other compared to people in most other professions. There are rivalries and tensions in every work place, but in the closed world of the ballet they can often be more obvious.

Preparations for the performance can start as far ahead as two hours before curtain-up. A few dancers are very lucky and have bodies which warm up quickly. Most have time for only a short break between the day's work and the preparation routine. There is the make-up to be done, which can vary from something simple in a modern work to something very complicated for a character role. The women have to get the hairstyles right, as well as sort out the piles of shoes every ballerina seems to collect. Some are good for one role, hopeless for another. Some are shiny, some are dull. Some just *feel* right.

A short warm-up barre will be given, not really a class in the proper sense, to get the body into gear for the show. Then, make-up might need retouching

A warm-up barre before the performance in make-up and ▶ head-dress.

Merle Park preparing her make-up for *Isadora*.

Last-minute adjustments to a tutu.

David Wall needs last minute attention to his costume and make-up before a performance of *Mayerling*.

before getting into a costume. There are always last-minute repairs to be done, small irritating things, like discovering that a hook or ribbon is missing. Wise dancers check that props they are going to use are in position or that doors and windows really do open and close properly. There may be time for a word with the conductor about the correct tempo or to go over a movement which is worrying the dancer with the ballet master.

While the audience is slowly filling the auditorium there is a frenzy of activity backstage. Then the faint sound of the overture comes through the heavy velvet curtain, and with a heavy sweep the curtain rises and the dancers are blinded by the fierce front-of-house lights.

For the audience there is the effortless magic of the dance. For the dancers there is the almost super-human effort to make the magic look effortless. The ballerina looks for a central light to 'spot' on while she turns, the corps de ballet concentrate on trying to keep straight lines, everyone is coping with an uneven or slippery stage, the Prince is trying to support the ballerina having just been hit by a stray piece of jewellery, the extras playing courtiers or guards try not to look embarrassed in costumes which do not fit.

Marguerite Porter collects her thoughts before going on stage.

Natalia Makarova seen from the wings during a performance of *Swan Lake*.

A quiet moment backstage for the two 'children' in *A Month in the Country* before their entrance.

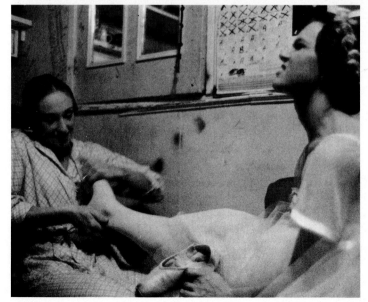

Lesley Collier gets some urgent attention to her foot from a colleague during a performance of *Les Sylphides*.

A helping hand waits in the wings as Mikhail Baryshnikov runs off with Lesley Collier held high in Frederick Ashton's ► *Rhapsody*.

With a final swish the curtain sweeps down and there is a thunder of applause. The company accept the cheers. The ballerina accepts the flowers. She kisses one and hands it to her Prince. More thunderous applause. Curtain down!

There may be a discussion of the performance with choreographer or conductor, but then there is the messy business of taking off the make-up and getting the costume back to the wardrobe. Then, after signing a few autographs at the stage door, very tired dancers either rush home or go out for a quick meal with friends from the company. They know that early tomorrow morning there will be that little matter of the daily class . . .

Baskets and bouquets after Frederick Ashton's *Jazz Calendar*.

Lesley Collier signs autographs at the stage door.

◀ Merle Park and a shower of flowers.

Although a dancer may have a good career in a major international company it is a very special lifestyle. While ordinary people can expect to work until they retire at the usual age, dancers always know at the back of their minds that their working life, as a dancer, is going to be short. Ann Nugent's career is a typical story of how dancers have to adjust both when dancing and after. This story has a happy ending, many do not, and it is a story which goes from . . .

Stage to Stage

I never knew where the need to dance sprang from. It was simply a part of me, so that when I was seven and went to my first performance – three short works by The Royal Ballet – something deep inside responded. It was as if ballet and I had already been introduced, there was no decision to be made, I just had to dance.

My parents, however, were not keen. They were concerned with guiding me towards a happy and secure future – and ballet demanded so much. It took years of pleading, until eventually, recognizing that my need was too strong to deny, they let me audition for The Royal Ballet Senior School.

But 14 was already too late, and the weekly classes at my convent school had not even begun to prepare me for the standard I should have achieved. I knew nothing of the seemingly advanced steps required at the audition. However the letter of rejection did not close all doors and so I tried for another school.

I auditioned for the Arts Educational School at Tring, to the north of London, and was accepted. This was the school that supplied the children for London Festival Ballet's production of *The Nutcracker*, and now it was to be my passport to the real world of ballet. For despite spending my pocket money on tickets for performances, pouring over dance books, magazines and my scrapbooks of cuttings, I was very far removed from it.

After the audition, as my mother and I left Arts Educational, I caught a glimpse of what was to come. We passed a studio and through a wall of glass saw a class of girls working at the barre. One stood in retiré with her arm in fifth position and a look of real fear on her face. For the first time I saw the struggle that had to be a part of ballet. It would no longer be a charming fantasy.

Indeed the shock of transferring to a theatre school proved far greater than I could have anticipated. From being the best in my class, I was suddenly as inadequate as if I had never danced before. Oh the struggle to co-ordinate and master the body, to stretch and strengthen the legs, to make the ankles firm for pointe work, and to let the arms conduct themselves gracefully on top of all that effort! It was a relief when someone told me the great teacher Cecchetti had said that the arms were the hardest thing of all to study.

My new teachers spoke of my 'beautifully pointed feet and good line', but were less enthusiastic about my achilles tendons. The wretched things needed special daily exercises to lengthen them, so as to improve first my demi-plié and then the all-important jump. But however hard I tried they still seemed pitifully tight. What had I done to deserve such misfortune!

Still, Arts was a happy school and looking back through old diaries I see that my whole day glowed if I won special praise for ballet. Equally it fell apart when I was found wanting! Ideas of stardom were lessening, but the driving sense of vocation was stronger than ever, and it never occurred to me to question my future prospects.

Schooldays were full of other subjects too, not least educational ones. In order to balance academic with vocational studies, we took our GCE (General Certificate of Education) exam instructions in two years. The range of subjects included English Language, Literature, Religious Knowledge, French, History, Geography and Art. No science, maths or Latin, which was a pity. Of course I did not mind at the time, but in retrospect it was unfortunate that transferring schools meant an end to Latin – for what an invaluable tool it is for writers.

As I had joined in the Lower Fifth, our first two work periods each day were academic, then came ballet, and after lunch two further sessions varying between modern stage dancing, tap, national, Greek, ballroom, drama mime or voice production. Other school subjects followed between tea and supper as well as time spent at prep, or what in day schools would be called homework. The junior and middle school days were divided into different shifts, so that we could all have our fair share of the school's four studios.

After supper on most evenings I hurried back to one of those same studios for my ritual practice, in the mistaken belief that if I did endless exercises, and repeated over and over again the class enchainements, there would be a miraculous improvement. Never mind analysis, quantity was the thing! Even then that was not the end, and further tests of strength had to be gone through in the dormitory. Nowadays, with more scientific knowledge of the body's capabilities, a quarter of those exercises done with detailed accuracy would have been more effective. Had I but known it, this was another of Cecchetti's sayings.

Rules at the school were strict. We had to dress neatly, wear grey housecoats, buttoned up over our leotards and tights, with blue belts fastened on top and our hair pulled back and fastened into a net and blue ribbons. Whenever we met the principals, Grace Cone and Olive Ripman, we were expected to drop meek little curtsies. It was in keeping with the necessary discipline.

After Tring I moved to the London branch of the school, where the student timetables (all individually planned to cope with varying standards) were new and exciting. I progressed to English and French at A (Advanced) level, History of Ballet, music appreciation and piano in the mornings. Ballet followed at 11 a.m., first of all in Royal Academy of Dancing and Cecchetti methods and, when I finally climbed up to 'company' class, to a freer more professional style. I also started to learn the classical repertory and pas de deux. Dancing with the boys was an exhilarating experience, and there was also the fun of having Errol Addison to teach us for these classes. He had danced with Diaghilev and was now a leading teacher. He never talked down to us as students, and we delighted in his repartee and vulgar jokes. Other professional dancers also came to teach us on occasions, and we were especially privileged to have classes from both Maryon Lane and Julia Farron as they were moving away from The Royal Ballet to full-time teaching.

Because of my single-minded absorption in ballet I was what my friends laughingly called 'a dedicated swan', and in keeping with my image I was suspicious of any form of contemporary movement, and positively loathed jazz dance. Once I turned up for a jazz lesson in pointe shoes, but the teacher missed the joke! My ideas were too narrow then but thankfully I never missed class, because later the barriers broke down and I actually enjoyed dancing in a musical.

During student years I had my first taste of professional work, appearing first in *The Nutcracker* and later in pantomime. It was an invaluable part of the training, for we could find out about make-up, costume-wearing and stage presentation at first hand.

Another lesson we learned was that the performance had to take priority over everything else – illness, injuries and broken hearts all had to be pushed into second place.

In the summer terms we had to compete in formal competition for cups in all our vocational subjects. I never rose above fourth place in ballet, which was not good for someone set on a ballet career! Ironically though I did better in other subjects, coming second once in Verse Speaking and actually winning a Music Cup.

Throughout the year we took exams in the different methods and forms of dance. Occasionally I did well, but more often than not I did not. Twice I failed my RAD advanced, then a week or two after the second failure I auditioned for London Festival Ballet and was handed a contract. (Clearly the examiners had been mistaken!)

Joining Festival Ballet was the height of my ambition, something almost too glorious to hope for. But fate has a strange way of juggling with ambition, and the company would not be the fulfilment of all my single-minded dedication, of all those years of tortuous training.

Three of us joined from Arts at the same time, travelling mid-week to join the company in Manchester in the north of England. It was a wet grey Wednesday, a bad omen perhaps. The company, whom we had known from *The Nutcracker*, seemed strangely distant: newcomers were resented.

Class on stage at the Palace Theatre, with only one light breaking through the gloom, was a let down after the previous day's airy studio. There were no more detailed corrections and it all seemed rather impersonal. Indeed we felt ignored, though we knew we were watched by unseen eyes, for everyone wanted to know what the 'new kids' were like.

Overnight we had to leave behind our student mentality and become more worldly wise, so that we could approach working in the theatre as if it were as natural as tea and toast. Our energy levels had to adjust to a class that was simply the prelude to a long day of rehearsals. But only after that did the real day begin as preparations started for the evening's performance. At 5.30 p.m. when the streets filled with office workers trudging wearily home, the dancers settled down to the serious art of make-up. The two hours to curtain up would rush by as we busied ourselves with sewing shoes, mending tights, washing rehearsal clothes, and warming-up again. Then the entire theatre came to life.

The three of us made our debut the following week in the northern resort of Blackpool, in *Swan Lake*. The moment of stepping onto so vast a stage, and not seeing anything beyond the orchestra pit because the lights dazzled, was overwhelming. Ben Stevenson, the evening's Prince stood beside the

Queen Mother's throne and made a joke, referring to us as three little maids from school. It went unheard by the audience, though not by us. We took it as a warm welcome.

The atmosphere backstage was mixed. In our corps de ballet dressing room some dancers were kind and helpful, others undeniably hostile. Professional jealousy I suppose. We were expected to learn their ways and their funny 'in' language, but to be over-familiar would mean instant disapproval.

Home comforts were forgotten during British tours as we had to put up with poor lodgings (digs) and, usually, long journeys to and from the theatre. But in compensation there were sunny tours to Europe, where we stayed in good hotels and enjoyed much local hospitality.

Work continued without a break. I loved Harald Lander's *Etudes*, but *Giselle* was another matter, particularly the Wilis in the second act. As the spirits of girls who died on their wedding nights we were on stage for most of that act in carefully rehearsed patterns, but it is absurdly difficult to keep in exact lines when you are new (later you develop a sixth sense about it) and I was always getting into trouble for being an inch or so out of place. I remember particularly the agony of long slow hops in arabesque across one of the widest stages in Europe at the San Carlos Opera House in Lisbon, and angry accusations hissed from the lips of another Wili as I wobbled. How I wished the floor would swallow me up!

Even so *Giselle* was rehearsed by Anton Dolin and that was quite a thrill, as was the presence of Margot Fonteyn who danced with us at some performances of *Swan Lake*. I never imagined that some years later I would work with her again, but in a quite different capacity. The company at that time was led by Galina Samsova, Lucette Aldous and John Gilpin and the joy of working with them was unforgettable. Equally unforgettable were the continuing practical jokes of Ben Stevenson (now Director of the Houston Ballet), whose heightened sense of the ridiculous lightened many a heavy working day.

For some dancers Festival Ballet was an admirable way of life, but it left me wanting something more, only I did not know what I was looking for until the company and I said an amicable goodbye and instead of finding another job I found Audrey de Vos, a wonderful teacher. She was more attuned to the harmony of movement and the workings of individual bodies than anyone I have known. She gave me the peace and fulfilment in dance that until then had been missing in my work. She brought out gifts so as to conceal weaknesses, and I even began to jump well!

I started performing again with small companies, and went to Scotland to work with Peter Darrell (now

Director of Scottish Ballet). Then I decided, like so many other English dancers, to audition in Europe. Gothenburg in Sweden, my first port of call, offered me a contract.

The great advantage of ballet is that there are no language barriers. Even though dancers may have different mother tongues, they share the language of dance in studios the world over. In Gothenburg the ballet company was made up of 13 different nationalities but there were no communication problems, and luckily our teachers and coaches mostly worked in English. What a bonus it was to live in a foreign land as a well-paid member of the community.

But although living conditions were good, the work was not entirely satisfactory because we had a dull repertory. Some of our new ballets had poor choreography, and even *Les Sylphides* was drained of its qualities because too many rehearsal directors tried to give it too many different interpretations! I almost preferred dancing with the opera company. To my astonishment I was cast in the final production of the year to tap and sing (in Swedish) in the musical *Cabaret*. Suddenly modern dance became fun, and how glad I was that my school had made me do it. However, it was not enough to keep me in Gothenburg. I was homesick, and also tired of what had turned out to be a second-rate ballet company. I could have stretched out my talent there until retirement, but it seemed more sensible to move on to another career while I was still young enough.

Doing what? That was the question! I thought, talked and looked. Then after a secretarial course, I found delightful jobs doing publicity for two publishers, first as assistant, then manager. For a few months I turned my back on ballet. I learned to drive, bought a car with my Swedish savings, and rushed off to every conceivable evening class in an effort to catch up with some of the things I had missed in the closeted world of ballet.

Soon ballet began to pull again. A performance by Northern Ballet Theatre stirred me into action. How unfortunate it was to see the wonderful dancing on stage, but so many empty seats in the auditorium. I had to do something about it, or try to. Assembling pen and paper I devoted a whole weekend to juggling with words, until I produced two pages that more or less said what I wanted to say and posted them to the local newspaper. Next morning the Arts Editor telephoned, apologizing that he could not use my piece because the performance had already been reviewed, but promising to put me on his panel of critics for the future.

I thought I would hear nothing more, but the following week he rang again and asked me to go and cover a play. I never asked what a critic's qualifications should be – just seized the opportunity and went. The opportunities continued.

My day-time career was progressing and I moved back into dance full-time, through a job in the dance department of the Arts Council of Great Britain. This provided an invaluable view of the dance scene, from Covent Garden to contemporary and experimental work. Here suddenly were whole new worlds of expression.

Then I was asked to go and work as an assistant to Margot Fonteyn in her beautiful home in London's fashionable Knightsbridge and I could hardly believe my luck, just eight years since I had been one of so many swans. She was warm, kind and full of fun.

Just at that time, and by another lucky chance, my brother bumped into an old school friend who happened to work for the British theatrical news-paper *The Stage*. Did they, he asked without prompting from me, need a dance critic? The reply came back that they could probably give work to a stringer, that is someone who deputizes for the regular critic when there is a clash of performances.

My first piece appeared in *The Stage* in 1978, and I have been writing for the paper ever since. Sadly the regular critic had to retire through illness and I took his place just as dance was burgeoning and the editor wanted (or would accept if I pushed him) a bigger and more thorough coverage of the field.

Then the magazine *Dance and Dancers* started asking me for contributions, and gradually my responsibilities escalated until I found myself writing about dance seven days a week! How strange it all is and yet I have never before been so happy and fulfilled in my work.

Writing, in its way, is quite as tough as dancing, only the hard work goes on in the brain which never seems to stretch far enough. A critic has to be able to examine and assess more than just the dance. Consider all the elements that go into a performance, music, story, set, costume design, overall production standards and you may imagine the difficulties of summing it up in a few hundred words.

How can any of us know enough to understand everything we see? The 'ballet eye' is a mixed blessing for it does not always serve the dance best if technical excellence is given priority over all the other aspects of a performance. The critic must have a thirst for knowledge, so as to grow within his or her chosen profession and keep an awareness of the delicate balance of everything that goes into a production. This for me is the great luxury of our work.

Although this is an introduction to ballet, it is always wise to remember that there are many other opportunities outside the great classical ballet companies. As you set out as a student you may not think of these but as you study and progress it is good for every young dancer to realize that outside the studio there is a . . .

World of Dance

Although this book is an introduction to the world of ballet it is impossible today to ignore the whole wide world of dance. Modern or contemporary dance is a major part of this. It is also important that you should not ignore it as the barriers which existed between ballet and modern dance are now almost completely broken down and many young dancers who train at a classical ballet school may find themselves either being expected to perform in modern works in a classical company or even taking up modern dance as a career.

The repertoire of a classical company such as the Royal Ballet includes works by modern choreographers such as Hans van Manen or Glen Tetley and working with classical dancers these choreographers have made their work a mixture of the two styles; a mixture in which it is very difficult to label the work either ballet or modern

Alexandra Radius and Han Ebbelaar in Hans van Manen's *Twilight*.

dance. It is also true to say that dancers in the classical tradition, trained in the system which has grown up over the years, have a wonderful body and a wonderful technique for the modern choreographer to work with. Often their range is much greater than a dancer who has trained in only one modern style.

Modern dance has a completely different history from that of the ballet; a history much more related to individual dancers than to one particular system of teaching and technique. In fact modern dance started as a battle by certain dancers and theorists against what they saw as the limited approach of the ballet. Their mistake, and I think they would all accept this today, is that they saw the discipline of the ballet class, the repetition of set exercises as limiting when it was really preparing the body in the best way possible to express what a choreographer wants. It was also a battle against the subject matter of the ballet and here, towards the end of the 19th century, they may have had a point. They felt strongly that the dance was not being used fully to express real emotions and was far too concerned with fairies, magic or just frivolity.

The move towards creating modern dance started in Germany in the middle of the last century with the work of Jaques-Dalcroze and his assistant Rudolf von Laban in their school at Dresden, now in East Germany. It is significant that neither were dancers; they were both professors who talked and wrote about the theory of dance.

The real movers of the art of modern dance came from America, though they had all been influenced by the Dalcroze/Laban teachings. The greatest name from this time, Isadora Duncan, wanted to free dance from restrictions and return to the natural beauty of Greek dance. Ruth St. Denis looked to the mystic East for her inspiration and created dances based on Indian temple dances. Isadora's free-flowing dances about passion and revolution are now almost lost as they were based on her personal style of movement and not on a system which would help keep them. Ruth St. Denis and her husband Ted Shawn, were in a way more influential as they founded the Denishawn School in Los Angeles which produced the people who really established modern dance both in the theatre and as a system of teaching. Most important of these has been Martha Graham and her success has in many ways overshadowed the work of people like Doris Humphrey, who apart from being a great performer, was also very important in expressing modern dance ideas in words.

Martha Graham was the most successful teacher and performer and her system is now the most common, though even she, in recent years, has moved a little towards the lightness and speed of classical dance. She has even choreographed a ballet, *Lucifer* for Margot Fonteyn and Rudolf Nureyev! The technique she evolved is widely used by schools and companies around the world, including the London Contemporary Dance Theatre, and she still directs her own school in New York at an age estimated to be somewhere around 87! Many of her partners and students are now influential choreographers and teachers, including Merce Cunningham, Alwin Nikolais and Paul Taylor. They have changed the technique to suit themselves and in this way modern dance remains a very personal form.

There are as many different modern classes as there are teachers, but the Graham Class contains many of the most common ideas. Graham has many personal ideas about why you should dance and how. She believes that all movements should be based on the way the body is made and not force it into the unnatural positions demanded by classical ballet. She also believes that the dancers should accept the force of gravity which pulls the body to the ground and not fight against it, as you will find in the classical school. A Graham class is divided into four main sections: exercises on the floor; exercises standing; exercises to jump; and exercises for falls, a very important part of Graham choreography.

Martha Graham as Mary Queen of Scots.

The floor exercises stretch the leg, but with the foot in its natural right-angle position and not straining to point. They also introduce another important Graham theory; that of contraction and release which is based on breathing. Inhaling is the release, exhaling, the contraction. The second part of the class involves exercises for feet, legs and hips and also introduces a modern form of plié in which there is a slight turn-out as in ballet. The third part of the class involves all the modern forms of jumps and leaps and the final part concentrates on fall and recovery. A Graham dancer must know how to fall to the ground in a variety of ways, with a knee-bend and falling backwards for example, and to a variety of rhythms.

Courses in modern dance are now almost as readily available as those for classical ballet and are particularly good for late starters who may enjoy dancing, but do not necessarily want to make a career of it. It is still possible, though, to start a modern dance career relatively late, especially for reasonably athletic boys. This has made modern dance particularly popular in colleges and universities as so many students are not only able to participate, but are also sympathetic to some of the more serious subjects modern dance has been used for.

In the early years of her career, during the 1920s and 1930s Martha Graham produced very intense works about personal relationships, but towards the end of her active career she became obsessed with Greek and other myths, producing a whole sequence of dances on these subjects, such as the story of Oedipus, in *Night Journey*, and a full-length *Clytemnestra*. These ballets have never had the same power since she stopped dancing the main role herself, but they are still very strong and great theatre, and are often shown on television.

Now there is a whole new young generation of modern dancers to whom even Martha Graham seems a bit old-fashioned. Some still believe in having real dance quality and exciting movement in their dances, like Paul Taylor or Twyla Tharp. Others seem to actually dislike anything you would recognize as dance, classical or modern, and produce works with little more than a bit of walking around or reading poetry or rearranging the decor.

A major source of employment for dancers is now on the stage and television, as well as in cabaret and films. In all these areas you will find that many of the dancers have been trained at the finest classical ballet schools, as well as the many schools offering all-round theatrical training. These schools are no longer as separate as they used to be. Just as modern dance and classical ballet have grown closer together, so have all other forms of theatre dance. No longer should you expect to train strictly for one dance form, an improvement which not only creates more complete performers, but also increases your chance of finding work in the crowded world of dance.

That all dance forms should come together is not really surprising when you think how many great choreographers from the ballet have worked on musicals and, in recent years, how ballet companies have invited choreographers from the musical theatre, such as Joe Layton, to create for them. In the 1930s George Balanchine worked on several musicals (as well as his famous dance for baby elephants) of which the most famous is *On Your Toes* for which he created *Slaughter on Tenth Avenue* which has become a regular feature of the repertoire of New York City Ballet. In 1983 the whole show has enjoyed a successful revival

Dancers from the American Dance Machine in the football team dance by Tommy Tune from *The Best Little Whorehouse in Texas* and *The Rich Kids Rag* by Bob Fosse.

starring the great ballerina Natalia Makarova partnered by George de la Pena. He is a very good example of how the two worlds meet, starting out as a student at the High School of Performing Arts in New York (famous as the home of *Fame*) and then moving over to the School of American Ballet. He did not graduate into New York City Ballet (which might have been expected, as this is regarded as the normal procedure) but instead chose American Ballet Theater where he rapidly became a soloist and danced many leading roles. Being chosen to play Nijinsky in the major film opened new possibilities for him as he had always been interested in acting, but apart from this it took him into the world of the musical and he partnered Lauren Bacall in *Woman of the Year*. He now finds himself starring in a Broadway musical partnering a great ballerina in a dance by one of ballet's greatest choreographers, staged by Peter Martins, another of today's great ballet stars!

Other major choreographers to work in the world of the musical have included Agnes de Mille and Jerome Robbins. Lee Theodore played the part of Anybody's in the original production of Robbins' *West Side Story* and when she realized that so many wonderful dances from these and other shows were often lost when the show closed, she set up the American Dance Machine to rescue them. They now have a large repertoire of dances on video tape, often recreated by the original choreographers or dancers from shows now almost forgotten, as well as recent popular favourites which may have had the same fate.

Wayne Sleep has made one of the most successful transitions from the classical ballet to the musical stage, though he still dances with the Royal Ballet in the virtuoso roles for which he is famous. A pupil of the Royal Ballet School, his outstanding technique and sparkling personality led to him dancing leading roles in the musicals *Cats* and *Song and Dance* and he now has his own dance company DASH. Here he is shown rehearsing and in a performance of *Song and Dance* by Andrew Lloyd Webber.

Ballet cannot exist by itself. Many other things go into each performance, such as the costumes, the decor, the music, the story. Each of these has a history of its own just like . . .

Music for Dance

In the early years of the ballet, in the age when great spectacles, such as the *Ballet Comique de la Reine* of 1581, took place in the courts of Europe, music was only a small part of the action. Mostly it would be in the form of quiet interludes composed for small groups of instruments, more like a chamber orchestra than a full symphonic orchestra, or as fanfares to herald the entry of decorated carriages which brought in the dancers. Many of the instruments used today had not been invented then, and the ability of the composers and players was very limited by modern standards. When you read stories about the fantastic and elaborate machines which were built to create special effects such as flying, as well as the animals which often took part, it is surprising that the music could be heard at all!

It was not until the middle of the 17th century, during the reign of Louis XIV of France, that music for ballet started to resemble what we know today. Louis helped the dance to develop and as he liked to dance himself. He encouraged his friend, the composer Jean-Baptiste Lully, to create new music for the dance sections of plays which were given at court, such as those written by Jean-Baptiste Molière. Lully introduced faster rhythms and brighter tunes, as well as dances such as the minuet which became very fashionable. As Lully was also a talented performer he directed the whole performance sometimes conducting by beating the ground with the end of a long staff, which cannot have helped improve the sound.

Although ballet and ballet music were becoming more important and popular, they were still usually part of a larger entertainment made up of singing, drama and spectacular scenic effects. It would still be almost a century before complete ballets using only dance, with some mime, would become accepted.

After Lully's death, Jean-Philippe Rameau created many works with very important ballet interludes, but they were still part of larger productions. In England you would find the same style, with dance being just one element of the great masques produced by such people as the playright Ben Jonson.

It was not until the middle of the 18th century when composers such as Christoph Gluck wrote really important pieces, like his *Don Juan,* for the ballet. Wolfgang Amadeus Mozart wrote *Les Petits Riens* and even Ludwig van Beethoven wrote a small amount of ballet music including *The Creatures of Prometheus*, though this was in a style already going out of fashion.

Then in 1789 Jean Dauberval choreographed *La Fille Mal Gardée.* This was a turning point in the world of ballet

as for the first time a complete story of 'real' people, not the gods and goddesses who had featured before, was put on the stage. Though the music is not important as *music*, it is important as the unknown composer took popular tunes of the day and fitted them very cleverly to the different characters and situations. Other ballet music at this time was still formal and did not really match the story, even when written by a great composer.

In the early years of the 19th century, during the period of ballet history known as the Romantic Age, ballets such as *La Sylphide* and *Giselle* were created. For a long time the music for these ballets has been regarded as unimportant, but if you listen closely you will know how clever it really is. Apart from being enjoyable, it also perfectly suits every scene and mood as well as fitting each character.

La Sylphide was first produced in Paris in 1832 with some rather sickly music by Jean Schneitzhoeffer. But when the great Danish choreographer August Bournonville created his own version of the ballet in Copenhagen in 1834 he could not afford to use the original music so he asked a young nobleman, Hermann von Løvenskjold to write a new score. He not only very cleverly worked in some tunes from the original, which Bournonville remembered from his time in Paris, but also for the first time, gave the characters theme tunes.

By the time we reach 1870, nearly 30 years after the end of the Romantic Age, both ballet and ballet music in France were having a bad time. The ballet was not regarded as a serious art and ballet music was just a collection of pretty tunes to help pass the time. But from this time comes one masterpiece, *Coppelia,* which is full of lively tunes and exciting national dances such as the mazurka and czardas.

The centre of the ballet world had moved from Paris to Russia and it was there that the next great age of ballet music would start, an age which would last well into the 20th century with the music of Igor Stravinsky. Music for ballets at the Tsar's Imperial Theatres was composed to order by staff musicians, the most famous being Ludwig Minkus, who held the post of Court Composer from 1864 to 1871. He produced rousing, thumping tunes as did the resident conductor, Ricardo Drigo. Though they created exciting ballets such as *La Bayadère* and *Don Quixote,* the music is almost interchangeable from one ballet to another and from composer to composer. If in doubt about the composer of a piece, call it Drinkus.

Peter Tchaikovsky was already a successful composer when he was asked to write the music for *Swan Lake* which had its first performance in 1877. It is hard to realize now that this much loved and most popular ballet was not a success. This was partly because of the bad choreography by Wenzel Reisinger (you will know the 1896 version by Marius Petipa), but also because the audience found Tchaikovsky's music difficult to accept. They thought it sounded too 'symphonic' and not at all like the 'Drinkus' they were used to.

Peter Tchaikovsky.

Other great composers of this period included Nicolai Rimsky-Korsakov and Alexander Glazunov who created *Raymonda* in 1898. Rimsky-Korsakov was very influential as a composer and teacher. He worked with Serge Diaghilev in the early years of Diaghilev's Ballet Russes and created *Scheherazade* for the 1910 season in Paris. On the same programme was *The Firebird* by the young Igor Stravinsky.

With Stravinsky, ballet music comes into the 20th century properly. The brilliance of *The Firebird* was soon followed by the pathos of *Petrouchka*. And then in 1913 *The Rite of Spring* burst into a startled world causing a riot in the theatre and a lasting change in the world of ballet music.

The artistic policy of Diaghilev attracted other great composers such as Claude Debussy and Maurice Ravel to work with the ballet, soon followed by Serge Prokofiev. Stravinsky remained the giant of ballet music until his death in 1971. In recent years there have not been many names which can be put alongside these as composers who have created specially for the ballet.

It is always best if a choreographer can work closely with a composer to create a new ballet, but often nowadays the problems of time and money mean that the choreographer is more likely to use a piece of music already written for some other purpose, such as an opera or a concert piece.

This gives the choreographer greater freedom and brings a wider range of music into the theatre. For instance, more people must have heard the music of modern composers such as Lutoslawski, at dance performances than in the concert hall. The price of this is that not much original ballet music is now written. Great choreographers such as Kenneth MacMillan invariably use scores made up from existing music, though he did ask Richard Rodney Bennett, famous among other things for his score for the film, *Murder on the Orient Express*, to write the music for *Isadora*. You are more likely to hear new music in one of the many workshop performances which often take place given by groups from the big companies, or at modern dance performances.

Some composers have a particular relationship with the ballet. Here are a few:

Adolphe Adam (1803–1856) was a French composer who wrote some of the most successful ballets of the middle 18th century including *La Fille du Danube* which is not seen any more and his masterpiece *Giselle*, which is one of the most-performed ballets today.

Alexander Borodin (1833–1887) was a Russian composer, but only in his spare time. He really worked as a Doctor and Professor of Chemistry, but although he did not compose much for the ballet he did write the marvellously exciting *Polovtsian Dances*, part of his opera *Prince Igor*.

Frederick Chopin (1810–1849) was a Polish composer who lived most of his life in Paris. Most of his music was written for the piano and although he did not have any direct connection with the ballet, Mikhail Fokine used several pieces for his ballet *Les Sylphides* one of the most famous 'white' ballets. Its original title, still used in Russia, was *Chopiniana*.

Aaron Copeland (1900–) is a very important American composer who has written much music specially for the ballet. Many of these pieces have had particularly 'American' themes, including *Appalachian Spring* for Martha Graham, *Billy the Kid*, which was choreographed by Eugene Loring, and *Rodeo* by Agnes de Mille.

Claude Debussy (1862–1918) was a French composer whose style was often compared to the impressionist style of painting. His most famous piece to be used for the ballet was *L'Après-midi d'un faune* (Afternoon of a Faun) which caused a riot at its first performance with choreography by Nijinsky.

Leo Delibes (1836–1891) was a French composer who created some sparkling music in his ballets *Coppelia* and *Sylvia* both of which are popular today. He was a student of Adam and his brilliant orchestration was said to have influenced Tchaikovsky.

Aram Khachaturian (1903–) is a Russian composer from the Republic of Armenia. He has used the strong folk rhythms of his native land in ballet music such as *Gayaneh*, but his most popular piece is *Spartacus* which includes a theme much used in television programmes.

Jean-Baptiste Lully (1632–1687) was born in Florence, but lived much of his life in France at the court of Louis XIV who appointed him Composer to the King in 1661 and director to the Académie Royale de Musique in 1672. He composed many ballets in plays by Molière and also included important ballets in the operas he wrote, starting a tradition which said that *every* opera presented at the Paris Opera had to have a ballet interlude; a tradition which lasted well into this century.

Serge Prokofiev (1891–1953) was born in the Republic of the Ukraine in Russia, but spent important early years in Paris where he was able to work for the Diaghilev Ballet writing music for *Chout* in 1921 and, most importantly, *The Prodigal Son* for George Balanchine in 1929. After he returned to Russia in 1933 his most important ballet music was for *Romeo and Juliet* which was rejected by the Bolshoi Theatre in Moscow as it was not socialist enough! First produced in Brno in Czechoslovakia in 1938 it was eventually produced in Leningrad in 1940 and Moscow in 1946, largely through the influence of the great ballerina Galina Ulanova. Other music includes *Cinderella* and *Peter and the Wolf* which has always been a popular piece with choreographers.

Maurice Ravel (1875–1937) was a French composer whose music was, like Debussy's, compared to impressionist painting. For the Diaghilev Ballet he wrote *Daphnis and Chloe*. Other pieces by him, such as the *Mother Goose Suite* and *La Valse,* have often been used by choreographers and his most famous piece, *Boléro,* originally specially written for the dancer Ida Rubenstein, has been used recently by choreographers as different as Sir Anton Dolin and Maurice Béjart.

Igor Stravinsky (1882–1971) was born in Russia and died in New York. He is buried in Venice close to the tomb of Diaghilev. He is the most important figure in ballet music of this century from his early pieces for the Diaghilev Ballet and continuing from his first work with George Balanchine in 1929, *Apollo* (then called *Apollon Musagète*), right up to his death. His ballets include *The Firebird, Petrouchka, The Rite of Spring, Pulcinella, Les Noces, The Fairy's Kiss, Card Game, Orpheus* and *Agon* and there are many others. To pay homage to this great musician George Balanchine organized the Stravinsky Festival of 1972 during which works were created to almost all the music he wrote.

Peter Tchaikovsky (1840–1893) wrote the music for the three great classic ballets, *Swan Lake, The Sleeping Beauty* and *The Nutcracker,* but much else of what he wrote has been used by choreographers ever since, as it is all so theatrical in feeling as well as being deeply emotional. Perhaps the most famous piece is *Serenade,* which was the first ballet George Balanchine created when he went to America, set to the *Serenade for Strings.* Tchaikovsky did not know the great success of his works in his lifetime. He liked *The Sleeping Beauty* best, but at the first performance the Tsar thought it was only 'very nice'. He was never very happy with *The Nutcracker,* though the music is so sparkling, as he found the story dull. He never lived to see the successful version of *Swan Lake* which was only produced the year after his death as a memorial, by Marius Petipa and Lev Ivanov who was responsible for the 'white' acts.

From left to right: Debussy, Ravel and Prokofiev.

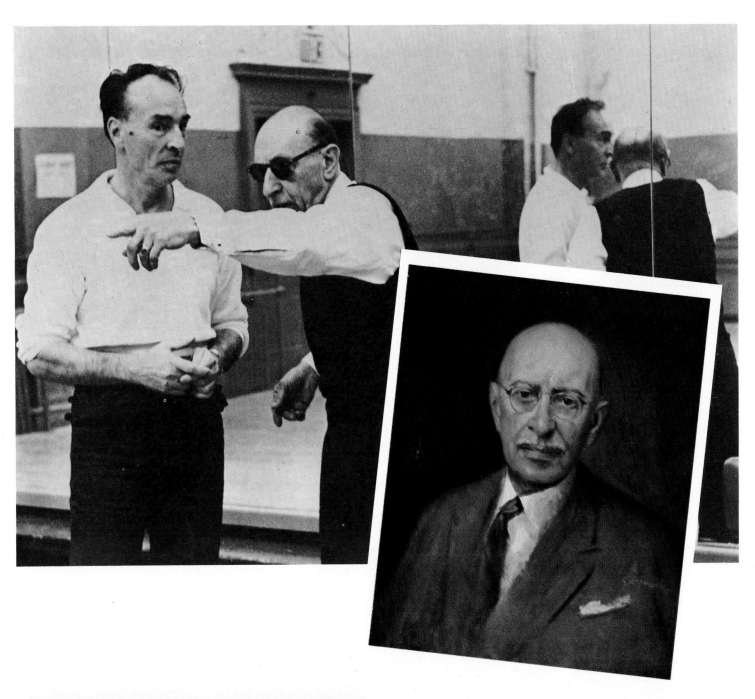

Igor Stravinsky, a formal portrait and a photograph of him with George Balanchine with whom he worked closely for over 40 years.

Kay Mazzo and Peter Martins of the New York City Ballet in a moment from *Violin Concerto*, one of the many ballets Balanchine created to Stravinsky's music.

The history of the ballet is shown very clearly when you study the gradual development over the centuries of both . . .

Decor and Costume

Ballet did not start in a theatre of the type we have today. It took place in the great ballrooms and courtyards of royal palaces and the people involved were not so clearly divided into dancers and audience. The whole performance was a great spectacle in which the courtiers took part alongside animals, fantastic machines to create special effects as well as the decorated food which was served at the banquets. The beautiful palaces of the time with their formal gardens gave a natural background to the performance to which the designers added waterfalls or lakes or mountains or clouds according to the story which was being told. The costumes would be the court dress of the period to which they would add decorations. The result, though fantastic to look at, did not make dancing very easy. Naturally the men in their doublets and hose had freedom to perform more complicated footwork, but the ladies were well covered with heavy skirts which touched the floor. At this time, the early 16th century, the steps were not very complicated anyway and were little more than variations on mannered walking. But soon new steps were invented or popular ones made more complex and as this progress took place so

costume changed. The most important change was shown in the way that ladies' dresses were slowly raised from the floor, perhaps the best-known and lasting example being shown in the painting of 'La Camargo' by Lancret in which her skirt is cut well about her ankles to show off the fast footwork for which she was famous. This change was also only possible as, by this time, the early 18th century, ballet was being performed by professional ballerinas and not court ladies for whom such dress was still quite improper. Throughout the century there was not a very great change in costume, though La Camargo's rival Marie Salle created ballets for herself wearing flimsy greek robes, but she had to leave Paris to do it! By the beginning of the 19th century when technique involved the first multiple pirouettes and the first sign of the ballerina rising onto pointe, the full skirt had been modified into the typical romantic tutu which you see on the Wilis in the photograph of *Giselle*. As technique became more sparkling this was soon modified into the classical tutu and from then on rapidly developed to the glorious costumes of the Diaghilev era, body tights for modern ballets and even ballets in the nude.

Opposite you can see the typical Romantic tutu and, below, Marguerite Porter as Odile, the Black Swan, in a classical tutu. Anthony Dowell models one of Leon Bakst's costumes created for Diaghilev in 1912 (*Le Dieu Bleu* originally danced by Nijinsky) and dancers of the Royal Winnipeg ballet look sleek and elegant in body tights. And then there are costumes which fit no category as you can see below with dancers of the Sadler's Wells Royal Ballet dressed as pea pods in Ashton's ballet *Pas des Legumes*

And finally we come to the people who wear the costumes, express the music and bring to life the steps created by the choreographers, the . . .

Dancers

It would be possible to fill a whole book with the life stories of famous dancers, so in making this selection I have concentrated on those who have made a particular contribution to the history of ballet. Sometimes this is because they were the first to perform a particular step; sometimes because they created a particular role. This means that you may not find your favourite dancer of today here as I have left out many who are now performing, either as stars at the top of their profession or exciting newcomers who may be the stars of tomorrow. You can find out much more about these yourself from ballet magazines or reviews of their performances in newspapers.

Alicia Alonso (1917–) was born in Cuba and studied in New York where she worked in Broadway shows, as well as with some of the infant American ballet companies. She became ballerina of American Ballet Theater in 1941 and was famous for modern ballets such as *Undertow* by Anthony Tudor, as well as for her interpretation of *Giselle* which was one of the finest of her generation. Incredibly she still dances this role with her own company, the Cuban Ballet, in Havana. For many years she suffered from partial blindness but in recent years has had an almost miraculous recovery.

Mikhail Baryshnikov (1948–) was born in Riga, capital of the Soviet Republic of Latvia and studied ballet in Leningrad under the famous teacher Pushkin, who also taught Nureyev. He won the Gold Medal in the Varna Competition in 1966 and again in Moscow in 1969. Although he became one of the brightest stars of the Kirov Ballet, he decided to leave Russia for the West in 1974 while he was on tour in Canada. He has an incredible technique and charming stage personality which was used cleverly by Sir Frederick Ashton when he created *Rhapsody* for him to dance at the Gala given in honour of Queen Elizabeth, the Queen Mother on the occasion of her 80th birthday. Though he has not had the same influence as a choreographer as Nureyev has enjoyed, he produced *The Nutcracker* for American Ballet Theater which he now directs. He had a particularly exciting partnership with Gelsey Kirkland, the unpredictable American ballerina. Her electric stage presence and brilliant technique gave their performances together an extra magic.

Carlotta Brianza (1867–1930) linked two generations of ballet history. Born in Italy where she became a famous ballerina, she worked in Russia and created the role of Aurora in *The Sleeping Beauty* in Leningrad in 1890. Thirty years later she played the role of the evil witch Carabosse when Diaghilev produced the same ballet for his company in London in 1921.

Marie-Anne Cupis de Camargo (1710–1770) better known as La Camargo, was born in Brussels where her father was dancing master. She became the greatest ballerina at the Paris Opéra famed for her speed and brilliant footwork from the time of her unexpected debut when she leapt onto the stage at the last moment in place of a dancer who had not appeared. She is credited with being the first woman to perform the entrechat quatre and dared to raise the hem of her full skirt to allow the audience to see it.

Fanny Cerrito (1817–1909) or Madame Cherrytoes as she was nicknamed, was one of the five great ballerinas of the Romantic Age at the beginning of the 19th century. She travelled greatly and was particularly popular in London. She was married for a time to Arthur Saint-Leon,

Mikhail Baryshnikov in *Rhapsody*.

choreographer of *Coppelia*, who created many ballets for her, but none have passed the test of time.

Alexandra Danilova (1904–) was a member of the small troupe of dancers which left Russia in 1924 with George Balanchine. They eventually joined Diaghilev's company and later went on to start American ballet. She was famous for her wide range of roles which included comedy, such as the Can-Can Dancer in Massine's *La Boutique Fantasque* and *Coppelia*, and the classics such as *Swan Lake*. She is now an important teacher and colleague of Balanchine in New York and recently appeared as the teacher in the film *The Turning Point*.

Anton Dolin (1904–) studied in Britain and was engaged by Diaghilev to appear as a page in *The Sleeping Beauty*. Three years later he joined the company and stayed, with short breaks, until Diaghilev's death in 1929. He created many famous roles, in particular the Gymnast in *Train Bleu*, but his major contribution to ballet was as the perfect partner. Of his many choreographies the most famous is the charming reconstruction of the *Pas de Quatre* in which four of the greatest ballerinas of the Romantic Age appeared together in London in 1845.

Anthony Dowell (1943–) is perhaps one of the greatest danseurs nobles that Britain has ever produced, combining effortless technique with elegant stage presence. As a child he studied at the school run by the actress Susan Hampshire's mother and then at the Royal Ballet School. As a member of the Royal Ballet he had a very special partnership with Antoinette Sibley which has just been renewed. Ashton created the role of Oberon in *The Dream* for him. He now dances all over the world, often partnering Natalia Makarova.

Fanny Elssler (1810–1884) was born in the not-very-romantic sounding town of Gumpendorf in Austria and became one of the two principal ballerinas of the Romantic Age. She was particularly famous for her dramatic ability and the naturalness of her dancing. She toured America in 1840, one of the first ballerinas to do so and had a great triumph; so great that she broke her contract with the Paris Opéra by staying there too long. She danced frequently in London, including many performances of *Giselle* from 1842 onwards. She also had great triumphs in Russia and gave her final performance in Vienna in 1851.

Margot Fonteyn (1919–) holds the rarely awarded title of Prima Ballerina Assoluta and a special place in the hearts of today's ballet lovers. Born in Britain she made her first stage appearance at the age of four, but received her first serious ballet training in Shanghai, where her father was working, from George Gontcharov who had escaped there from Russia with Vera Volkova. On her return to Britain she took classes with Serafina Astafieva and then the Vic-Wells School. She was soon dancing with the young company (as a Snow-Flake in *The Nutcracker*) and working with Frederick Ashton. This close association was to continue through the years which saw her rise to her present position of eminence. She succeeded Markova as Ballerina of the Vic-Wells Company and by 1939 had danced

Odette-Odile, Giselle and Aurora, which became her most famous classic role. Ashton continued to create works for her including *Ondine* in which she danced the water nymph, and later, when she had formed the unforgettable partnership with Nureyev, *Marguerite and Armand*. She has recently introduced ballet to an even wider audience through her television series *The Magic of Dance* and continues her work as President of the Royal Academy of Dancing.

Margot Fonteyn as Ondine.

Christopher Gable (1940–) is now best-known as an actor, but during his years with the Royal Ballet he played an important role in establishing the importance of the male dancer. Indeed he could draw enormous audiences to the Royal Opera House at the time of Nureyev's arrival in the West. A pupil of the Royal Ballet School, he soon rose through the ranks of the Royal Ballet Touring Company (now the Sadler's Wells Royal Ballet) to become a Principal dancer and create important roles such as the Cousin in MacMillan's *The Invitation* and the Young Man in Ashton's *The Two Pigeons*. His partnership with Lynn Seymour reached a peak of emotional perfection when MacMillan created *Romeo and Juliet* for them. Troubled by injuries he gave up dancing and was then seen in films such as Ken Russell's *Tchaikovsky* and *The Boy Friend*. He now heads the new Central School of Dance in London.

John Gilpin (1930–) studied at the Cone-Ripman School (now Arts Educational) and joined Ballet Rambert in 1945 when it was a classical company. After a short period in Paris with Roland Petit, he joined London Festival Ballet and it was with this company that he achieved his greatest successes, becoming Director in 1962. He was the most stylish classical virtuoso of his generation in Britain, with an unforced and elegant technique. He is now an important teacher and coach and has written his autobiography, *A Dance with Life*.

Lucile Grahn (1819–1907) was the pupil of the Danish choreographer August Bournonville who created *La Sylphide* for her in Copenhagen in 1836. Soon after she had a disagreement with him and left for Paris and an international career which also took her to St. Petersburg and London; she was one of the four ballerinas who danced the *Pas de Quatre* there in 1845. She retired in 1856, but continued to work as Ballet Mistress in Munich. In gratitude for her last gesture, leaving her fortune to the city's poor, you will find a street named after her there.

Marcia Haydee and Richard Cragun, stars of John Cranko's Stuttgart Ballet in *Requiem*, which was created by MacMillan in memory of Cranko

Robert Helpmann (1909–) was Margot Fonteyn's partner during her important early years with the Vic-Wells Ballet. Quite early on, while still dancing and choreographing such ballets as *Hamlet*, he started acting and later made a career in films. Soon after the founding of the Australian Ballet in 1962 he returned to his native country Australia, and in 1965 became co-director of the company with Peggy van Praagh. He still appears in character roles and can be seen in the title role in the film of Nureyev's *Don Quixote*. For many years his celebrated partnership with Frederick Ashton as the Ugly Sisters in *Cinderella* was the high point of the Christmas season in London.

Zizi Jeanmaire (1924–) is one of an important group of excellent ballet dancers who brought ballet to a wider audience through films and popular shows in the 1940s and 1950s. She studied at the School of the Paris Opéra Ballet and joined the company in 1939. In 1944 she left to work with Roland Petit, whom she married. He created such dramatic roles as *Carmen* for her and she recently filmed it with Mikhail Baryshnikov. Her long legs and very short hair style became famous in films such as *Hans Christian Andersen*, with Danny Kaye, as well as in cabaret. She still appears on the ballet stage, usually in ballets created around her by her husband, for their company in Marseilles.

Karen Kain (1951–) is the outstanding Canadian Ballerina of today, with a wide international reputation. She is the first student of the School of the National Ballet of Canada to reach such heights, winning a silver medal as a soloist in Moscow in 1973, as well as first place in the pas de deux section with her partner Frank Augustyn. She has had many roles created for her and danced Terasina in the first performance of Peter Schaufuss's new production of *Napoli*.

Tamara Karsavina (1885–1975) was one of the outstanding pupils of the Imperial Ballet School in St. Petersburg at the turn of the century, graduating in 1902. She joined Diaghilev when he took his company to Paris in 1909 and formed a special partnership with Vaslav Nijinsky. Though she remained connected with the Imperial Ballet until the Russian Revolution of 1917, she will best be remembere remembered for the roles she created, including the Doll in *Petrouchka*, the Girl in *Le Spectre de la Rose* and the Firebird. She settled with her husband in Britain and was important in the setting up of the Royal Academy of Dancing as well as in helping dancers such as Fonteyn with their roles. She also helped Ashton with the mime in the second act of *La Fille Mal Gardée* from her memories of the production in St. Petersburg, providing a link across a century and a half through only four people. Her autobiography *Theatre Street*, mostly about her life in the Imperial School, is one of the most charming you can find.

Irina Kolpakova (1933–) was one of the last pupils of the teacher Vaganova who had been a ballerina in the Imperial Ballet of St. Petersburg before the Russian Revolution. After it she stayed in Leningrad (as St. Petersburg was renamed) and helped keep alive the classical tradition. Many of Kolpakova's roles have been filmed recently, in particular Raymonda, and in them you can see the pure Kirov style. She has also created some modern roles in ballets such as *The Stone Flower* and *Legend of Love*.

Serge Lifar (1905–) was the last great male star of the Diaghilev Ballet, who had a marvellous stage presence and was exceptionally handsome. In the last years of the Diaghilev Company up to 1929 he created such famous roles as Apollo and the Prodigal Son in Balanchine's ballets and when the company disbanded after Diaghilev's death he eventually became Director of the Paris Opéra Ballet and, with one short break, was a great influence there for almost 20 years. Though many of his ballets centred around himself, he also encouraged a whole generation of ballerinas including Nina Vyroubova and, most importantly, Yvette Chauviré. His choreography has not lasted, but his personal style is now part of the French style of dance.

Emma Livry (1842–1863) has a small but tragic place in the history of ballet. She was picked by Marie Taglioni to carry on the Romantic tradition and she choreographed *Le Papillion* for her in 1860. Unfortunately while Livry was rehearsing a mime role in an opera in 1862 her dress caught fire and she was very badly burned. She lingered on for almost a year and with her horrible death it can be said that the Romantic Age finally came to an end.

Karen Kain and Frank Augustyn in *La Fille Mal Gardée*.

Natalia Makarova (1940–) was a pupil at the Kirov School in Leningrad and graduated into the company in 1959. Her debut in *Giselle* came soon after and, although an unusual interpretation, it is a role she is particularly famous for. She also has a sparkling technique and phenomenal jump, best shown off in pas de deux such as *Don Quixote*. In 1970 she decided to stay in the West during a Kirov Ballet tour, joining Nureyev and Baryshnikov. She has danced a lot with American Ballet Theater as well as producing the full-length *La Bayadère* for them.

Dame Alicia Markova (1910–) is one of the most important figures in ballet in the West and Britain in particular. She studied with Astafieva in London and was discovered by Diaghilev at the age of 14. She joined his company at 16 and created the role of the Nightingale in Balanchine's ballet. After Diaghilev's death in 1929 she danced with all the young British ballet companies such as Ballet Rambert and the Vic-Wells, becoming ballerina there in 1933. She was the first British ballerina to dance Giselle and Odette/Odile and her style influenced a generation of other dancers especially in the Romantic ballets such as *Giselle*. During the war years in America and before, she was partnered by Anton Dolin and out of their concert groups grew London Festival Ballet. After her retirement she became very active in teaching, coaching and producing ballets with which she had been particularly associated, such as *Les Sylphides*.

Peter Martins (1946–) has very successfully combined two different schools of dance. He was a student of the Royal Danish Ballet School in his home town of Copenhagen and joined the Royal Danish Ballet in 1965. He was soon dancing the major Bournonville roles as well as modern ones. These included Apollo and it was after dancing some guest performances of this that he joined New York City Ballet. He has since developed into a very *American* dancer and has inspired Balanchine to create many important ballets for him. He has a particularly noble style, perfectly suited for Princes, but equally at home in Balanchine's ballets. He has had a great partnership with Suzanne Farrell who also inspired Balanchine to create

wonderful ballets. In 1983 he was appointed Ballet Master of the New York City Ballet.

Arthur Mitchell (1934–) studied at the School for the Performing Arts in New York, which has now become world famous through the film and television series *Fame*. He worked mostly in modern dance until he joined the New York City Ballet in 1956 becoming its first black Principal Dancer in 1959. He created roles in Balanchine's *Agon* and *A Midsummer Night's Dream*. In 1968, influenced by the death of Martin Luther King he decided to work with black children and opened a school in Harlem, New York, which has grown to an enormous size. He now devotes all his time to the school and the Dance Theatre of Harlem which grew out of it. This company is very popular with audiences on its many tours.

Vaslav Nijinsky (1888–1950) has possibly the most brilliant and most tragic story in the whole of ballet history. The brightest pupil at the Imperial Ballet School in spite of his rather oriental looks and unusual physique, he made a brilliant debut into the Imperial Ballet and while in the corps de ballet danced principal roles in *Paquita, La Fille Mal Gardée* and other ballets. It was about this time that he met Diaghilev with whom he was to enjoy a close working and personal relationship. Diaghilev guided him as a dancer in such famous roles as the Golden Slave in *Scheherazade*, and Petrouchka. After astounding audiences with his dancing he went on to astound them even more with his choreography which was completely different from anything they had seen before. *Afternoon of a Faun* in 1912 was booed at so much that Diaghilev ordered it to be danced again immediately; *Rite Of Spring* in 1913 caused a complete riot in the theatre. The combination of Stravinsky's violent music and Nijinsky's unusual choreography was too much for the Parisian audience. But by this time Nijinsky was already showing signs of the mental illness which would bring his career to an end by 1917. In 1913 he married Romola Pulszky and was banished from the Diaghilev company. She was to support him for 35 years through great troubles, when they had to move about the world almost as stateless people. He died in London in 1950 and in 1953 his body was moved to Paris to lie next to that of the grave of Auguste Vestris. (See page 95).

Rudolf Nureyev (1938–) made his celebrated leap for freedom in Paris in 1961 and immediately became one of the greatest influences upon ballet in the West as well as one of its most outstanding dancers. Born into a poor family he first studied folk dancing in the town of Ufa and at an early age gave lessons to help support his family and, more importantly, help his own studies of ballet with teachers from the local opera house. He was a very determined young man and while in Moscow managed to obtain an audition with the Bolshoi school. He was offered a place, but he knew that without a higher grade he could not hope to keep himself in Moscow, so he took a train to Leningrad, auditioned for the Kirov school and was accepted. He made rapid progress with his special teacher, Alexander Pushkin. At the time of his defection, he was one of the Kirov's brightest young stars, but had already been in trouble with

the authorities. He made his decision to escape and once in the West worked closely with Erik Bruhn, one of the greatest male dancers and very soon met Margot Fonteyn. Their partnership both in classic ballets such as *Giselle*, as well as the ballets specially created for them such as *Marguerite and Armand* by Frederick Ashton, had a special magic and gave Fonteyn a whole new career. He soon started to choreograph and his production of *La Bayadère* for the Royal Ballet was a ballet landmark. His dancing inspired a whole generation of male dancers. He is now Director of the Paris Opera Ballet.

Merle Park (1937–) ballerina of the Royal Ballet was born in Rhodesia (now Zimbabwe) and studied in Britain at the Elmhurst School before joining the Royal Ballet in 1954, becoming a ballerina in 1959. She is famed for her superb technique, light and fast, which was used best in ballets such as *La Fille Mal Gardée* and *The Sleeping Beauty*. She danced the ballerina role in Nureyev's *The Nutcracker* and has often been partnered by him abroad. Kenneth MacMillan created *Isadora* for her, which made full use of her dance and dramatic abilities. From 1983 she will bring the benefit of her experience to a new post, Director of the Royal Ballet School, though she will still appear at the Royal Opera House with the Royal Ballet.

Nureyev in Paul Taylor's *Aureole*.

Anna Pavlova (1881–1931) might possibly be thought the most important person in modern ballet after Diaghilev, as she was not only a supreme artist dancer on the stage, but a determined business woman who took ballet to places it had never been before: across America, across Australia and New Zealand, and even to Japan. A brilliant student at the Imperial School in St. Petersburg, she made a memorable debut in *Giselle* in 1903 and became a ballerina in 1906. Though she worked with Diaghilev in his first Paris seasons she soon broke away to form her own company. She was not as adventurous as Diaghilev and only danced very old-fashioned ballets. Even the new ones which were created for her were in the old style, but this was a style which her audiences found acceptable and which suited her. On her tours she inspired many people to take up dance, including the young Frederick Ashton who saw her in South America. Her company was made up of many British girls, though most hid behind Russian names, which was the fashion at the time, and after Pavlova's death it was many of these who set up ballet schools all over England, as well as around the world, starting the ballet boom we have today. She died in The Hague in 1931, having made her home for many years at Ivy House in London. This is now a Pavlova Museum, full of mementoes of her life and career.

Nadia Pavlova in *Giselle*.

Nadia Pavlova (1956–), today's Pavlova, was trained in Perm in Russia and while still a student won the Gold Medal in the Moscow Competition in 1973, partnered by Vyacheslav Gordeyev who is now her husband. Of the young generation of Russian dancers she has the most spectacular technique, charming personality and greatest dramatic ability and had already danced *Giselle* and *Coppelia* before she joined Moscow's Bolshoi Ballet in 1975. She can be seen in the film of *The Bluebird*.

Maya Plisetskaya (1925–) was the greatest ballerina to follow in Ulanova's footsteps at the Bolshoi Ballet. A very strong technical dancer she graduated from the Bolshoi School straight into the company as a soloist in 1943 and immediately danced important roles. She made a great impact when the Bolshoi Ballet toured the West for the first time and since then has often appeared with Western companies such as Maurice Béjart's Ballet of the Twentieth Century. She is married to the composer Schedrin who wrote the ballet *Carmen Suite* (not to be confused with Petit's *Carmen*) for her. After Ulanova's retirement she became Prima Ballerina Assoluta and also started to choreograph, in particular *Anna Karenina*.

Lynn Seymour as Anastasia.

Noella Pontois (1943–) was trained at the Paris Opéra Ballet School joining the corps de ballet of the company in 1961. By 1968 she was an *étoile* and had danced as a guest with London Festival Ballet and with Nureyev. She combines everything that is good about the French school of dance; lightness, speed, classicism and chic.

Peter Schaufuss (1949–) is not only an important Danish dancer, but in recent years has started to produce up-to-date versions of the old Danish ballets made by Bou Bournonville in the first half of the last century. His production of *La Sylphide* for London Festival Ballet won both the major ballet awards in the same year and his *Napoli* for the National Ballet of Canada was acclaimed by the critics and a great success with the public. He is producing *Folk Tale* for the Berlin Opera Ballet and has hopes to recreate Frederick Ashton's *Romeo and Juliet* in which his mother, Mona Vangsaae was Juliet, with his father, Frank Schaufuss as Mercutio, when it was first produced in his home town, Copenhagen, in 1956.

Lynn Seymour (1939–) is perhaps the greatest dramatic ballerina the Royal Ballet has produced. Born in Canada she studied there and in London at the Sadler's Wells School. After a short time with the Covent Garden Opera Ballet she joined the Royal Ballet Touring Company in 1957 moving to Covent Garden a year later. She was almost immediately selected to work with Kenneth MacMillan and she inspired him to produce his great ballets *The Invitation, Romeo and Juliet*, and in 1967 in Berlin, the one-act *Anastasia* which is now performed in the full version by the Royal Ballet. She also was the inspiration for Ashton to create *Two Pigeons* and *A Month in the Country*. Now retired from the Royal Ballet she can be seen dancing rock ballets or teaching.

Moira Shearer (1926–) will always be best known for her part in the film *The Red Shoes* which is still the best ballet film ever made. After studying at various schools she joined the Sadler's Wells Ballet in 1942 and within two years was a ballerina. Exceptionally beautiful, with a marvellous technique and wonderful line she was the only true rival to Fonteyn during the 1940s and created Ashton's *Cinderella* in 1948. In the same year she made *The Red Shoes* and became an international star, and possibly brought ballet to its biggest ever audience. After this she concentrated on an acting career, though she still danced occasionally. Since then she has made varied appearances including introducing the Eurovision Song Contest and is now working with the BBC as an announcer.

Michael Somes (1917–) after a career as an outstanding male dancer during the 1930s and 1940s made an important contribution to British ballet as Margot Fonteyn's partner when Robert Helpmann left the Sadler's Wells company. His striking presence and perfect partnering were a model to the next generation including David Blair (who succeeded him as Fonteyn's partner), Christopher Gable and David Wall. He is still a great influence in the company carefully looking after both the great classics and the Ashton ballets in the repertoire.

Marie Taglioni in *La Sylphide*.

Marie Taglioni (1804–1884) was a skinny and not very attractive child who was turned into the greatest ballerina of the Romantic Age by the hard work of her father, Filippo. After years of careful training she made her debut at the Paris Opéra in 1827 and was an immediate success through her exceptional lightness which made it look as though she was flying. At this time ballerinas did not stand on their pointes in the same manner as today; just up on tip-toe for a fleeting moment to make it look as though they were. In 1831 she appeared as a ghostly nun in the ballet scene of the opera *Robert the Devil* and with this ballet the Romantic Age, concerned with haunted woods, exotic countries and magical stories, was born. In 1832 her father created *La Sylphide* for her and she went on to conquer Europe, including Russia, where ballet fans were so excited by her performance that they cooked and ate one of her shoes after a performance! She appeared in London in the 1845 *Pas de Quatre*, undisputed Queen of the ballet, while the other ballerinas argued about the order in which they should appear ('Let the oldest dance first' said the producer, which put a stop to all discussion!). In her later years she lost much of the fortune she earned

and taught dancing and deportment to society ladies in London, finally retiring to Marseilles.

Galina Ulanova (1910–) had a special magic which was captured in the Russian film of *Romeo and Juliet*. She was never noted for a strong technique, but had great artistry, musicality and dramatic ability which more than made up for this. A student in Leningrad where her father was a dancer and ballet master she was taught by Vaganova and after joining the Leningrad Academic Theatre company in 1928 (later called the Kirov), soon danced the Bluebird Princess and Aurora in *The Sleeping Beauty* as well as *Giselle*. It was to show off her special qualities that the direction of the Bolshoi Theatre in Moscow finally allowed a production of *Romeo and Juliet* with Prokofiev's music to be staged and this is perhaps her greatest role. From 1959 she started to retire gradually and became ballet mistress at the Bolshoi as well as helping young ballerinas, especially Maximova, with the interpretation of roles with which she was associated.

Auguste Vestris (1760–1842) was a great dancer at the moment in ballet history when male dancing started to take the shape it has today. Costumes were changing in style and more exciting steps were added to the technique. He was the son of Gaetano Vestris (1729–1808) an Italian dancer who studied at the Paris Opéra, where his talents earned him the title 'God of the Dance' and had worked with the teacher Noverre who wanted to free dance from many restrictions including the use of masks and too much mime. Gaetano also excelled in quick jumps and the pirouette which was only just being perfected, in fact it is said that the German ballerina Anna Heinel, who bore him another son Apollon, was the first ballerina to perfect it. Auguste further perfected many of the steps in particular jumps and taught many of the next generation of dancers and choreographers including Bournonville.

Edward Villella (1936–) is one of the most influential of American male dancers of recent times, bringing ballet to a wide audience and making it an acceptable occupation for boys to take up. Much good work in this direction had been done by his fellow member of New York City Ballet, Jacques d'Amboise (who also appeared in such films as *Seven Brides for Seven Brothers*), but Villella had the benefit of much greater television coverage and a range of roles to show off his wonderful, sporty-looking technique. One of the greatest dancers of the role of the Prodigal Son, Balanchine also created the Rubies section of *Jewels* for him.

Virginia Zucchi (1847–1930) was one of the brilliant Italian ballerinas who were largely responsible for bringing new life to the ballet in Russia during the time when Petipa was the ballet master of the Imperial Ballet, a period roughly taking up the last half of the 19th century. In particular, she influenced the group of balletomanes, including Benois and Diaghilev, who started the new wave of ballet at the turn of the century. (The other great ballerina was Pierina Legnani who had a similarly strong technique and was the first ballerina to perform the famous 32 fouettés, in *Cinderella*. She also created the roles of Odette/Odile in *Swan Lake* in 1895.)

Useful addresses

The Royal Academy of Dancing
48 Vicarage Crescent, London SW11 3LT
Telephone: 01-223 0091

Imperial Society of Teachers of Dancing
(The Cecchetti Society and Imperial Ballet)
Euston Hall, Birkenhead Street, London WC1H 8BE
Telephone: 01-837 9967

96

Photographic Acknowledgments

Clive Boursnell 2, 3, 8–23, 55, 56, 57, 59–73, 88, Back cover;
Costas 34 top right and left; Anthony Crickmay 33, 90;
Jesse Davis 86, 87 top right, 88; Barry Gray 35, 89 top left;
Chris Nash 81; Novosti 91; Linda Rich 1, 29–32, 36–53;
Leslie Spatt 94; David Street Front cover, 6, 79, 96;
Martha Swope 78, 85; Darryl Williams, 25, 87 top left, bottom.